FINDING YOUR WAY

NAVIGATING YOUR FUTURE BY UNDERSTANDING YOUR LEARNING SELF

Christine A. Johnston

For information:

Let Me Learn, Inc
31 Driftwood Court
Glassboro, NJ 08028
Email:info@letmelearn.org

Printed in the United States of America
Library of Congress Cataloging-in-Publication Data

Johnston, Christine A.
    Finding Your Way: Navigating Your Future by Understanding Your Learning Self
    Collegiate Edition

Includes bibliographical references and index.

ISBN: 1456311077
ISBN 13: 9781456311070
1. Learning 2.Learning behaviors
Library of Congress Control Number: 2010916226
CreateSpace Independent Publishing Platform, North Charleston, SC
Bisac: Non-fiction/ self help/ collegiate

Production Editor: Linda C. Bateman

Typesetter: Tammy West

Cover and Graphic Designer: Beth Davis

Dedication

This book is written on the occasion of the Let Me Learn Processes'® Twentieth Anniversary and is dedicated to Emily, Noah, and Connor Johnston—in the hope that they will find their True North, navigate the global crosswinds of the 21st century, and use their individual Compass Roses to find Safe Harbor anchored in a rich and fulfilling life of learning

Acknowledgements

There are a number of people who have helped me find my way in life: my parents whose spiritual nurturing led me to find my True North, my husband and dearest friend, Dale, who has kept me on course when work and life circumstances sought to compromise my True North and diminish the use of my Compass Rose, and Bob Kottkamp, who first took me sailing and then helped me explore how understanding learning can make a difference for a lifetime.

Table of Contents

List of Figures, Tables, Worksheets

List of Figures, Tables, Worksheets

Foreword

When I was introduced to the Let Me Learn Process almost ten years ago, I was serving as the director of a career and academic planning center for a mid-sized state university. I immediately saw LML's potential for providing a degree of self-awareness to students that I had not found in other resources. Primarily I saw its power to help students achieve greater academic success, a more fitting career selection, stronger employment skills, and healthier personal dynamics with others.

I want the same power of awareness for you. I want you empowered and ready to navigate your future. Whether you are entering college as a first year student, a transfer, a re-entering student, or first-time adult learner, you are about to begin a journey that will change your life in meaningful ways. Along the journey you will be faced with weighty decisions. Your first is to choose a career goal that matches your interests and talents. That choice is quickly followed by others including selecting a major that prepares you for your chosen career, obtaining work experience to prepare for your career, and actually obtaining a position that will give you an opportunity to create a meaningful life.

If you are feeling a little anxious at this point, you are experiencing a normal response to the challenge of finding your way as an adult in a complicated world. The college experience is intended to help you make these choices and to equip you to develop your knowledge, skills, and talents to thrive and contribute to the career you choose. The college experience will also provide you with the resources to explore various career paths.

Using the tools found in this text is one way to prepare you to begin your journey—to help you find your way. It will do so by helping you navigate the realities of the educational institution in which you find yourself. In other words, it will help you understand yourself as a learner and equip you to gain the very most from the courses, classes, tests, and projects you will be completing. It will provide you with a strong sense-of-self that sees the journey as one of preparation for the career goal you have set for yourself. This knowledge of yourself will help you tweak your goal, re-visit your career choice, and refine your job skills.

I do not make these statements lightly. I have written the foreword to *Finding Your Way: Navigating Your Future by Understanding Your Learning Self*, as someone who believes in the value, importance, and power of its message. I believe the basis of the book, the **Let Me Learn Process**®, is truly an advanced learning system that both engages and empowers individuals. I believe that by understanding yourself as a learner you can grasp your vision, your True North, make discerning career decisions, and strategically navigate your future to achieve your life goals.

As you begin or continue your experience in higher education, you will have many opportunities for growth and development. However, I believe that none will be more powerful or have more potential to impact as many aspects of your life as what you will discover in *Finding Your Way*. Enjoy this wonderful journey!

Betsy McCalla Wriggins, BS & MS, University of Tennessee

Director (ret.), Career and Academic Planning Center, Rowan University

Past President, NACADA, The Global Community for Academic Advising

Who and What are setting the Course for Your Future?

A dear friend's father refers to the female voice of his global positioning system (GPS) as "the lady of the universe" (LOTU). It is the LOTU who guides his travel, helping him arrive at his destination in a safe and timely fashion. Wouldn't each of us appreciate having a lady of the universe to guide our decisions and to set us on a well-mapped career pathway? Which one of us wouldn't appreciate having warnings that alert us to any miscues in life direction or of any problems ahead?

While the features on our phones and vehicles provide all types of guides and technical assistance to keep us headed in the right direction, what type of resources do we have to guide us when making long term life decisions? What is the make-up of our personal GPS? Where is the voice of the LOTU when we need help navigating or recalculating our personal and professional lives?

The technology available to answer these questions is not one that needs to be purchased. It lies within each of our internal directional forces known as your Learning Patterns. This text was written for the express purpose of introducing you to these powerful internal resources and to help you use them with intention to plan your future, to plot your coordinates, and to navigate your life journey.

Truly, finding your way as a learner is a major challenge in life. The purpose of *Finding Your Way: Navigating Your Future by Understanding Your Learning Self* is to help you meet that challenge.

Do I Really Need to Find My Way?

The intended audience for this book is quite varied. Some individuals may have been stellar high school students, community college graduates, or military trainees who seek to enhance their learning skills. After all, what is the well-known adage?

"Chance favors the prepared mind."

—Louis Pasteur (Kounios, J., & Jung-Beeman, M., 2006).

Some intended readers may be adults who struggled in school and remain bewildered and haunted by those experiences, fearful of reentering the world of continuing education. Others may have hated school, endured it as a necessary evil, but who, having survived that dreadful experience, soared as problem solvers and entrepreneurs in the arena of life. In fact, the pattern of *failure in school and success in life* is quite common—and if you read on, you'll discover why.

Finally, this book is written especially for those who are still searching for a way to make learning work for them; those who are dissatisfied with their academic achievement; and those who seek greater self understanding to change, grow, and achieve better results.

A Guide to Navigating the Text

Finding Your Way is structured to guide you on an interactive and personal journey. You will discover how to use your mind with intention—that is, with a consciousness of what you are doing and why you are doing it—to absorb information and develop skills and judgment through self-directed assessment and personal reflection. Throughout the book you will be introduced to a new vocabulary that allows you to express yourself in specific terms as you learn to navigate life using your Directional Learning Forces or Learning Processes (See Glossary). You will note that throughout the text the words, "Learning Patterns," "Learning Processes," "Directional Forces," and "Directional Learning Processes," are used interchangeably.

Each chapter begins with a bulleted focus statement followed by **The Story**, which brings the focus of the bulleted statement into your personal life context. It is followed by **The Learning**, an extension of the focus that addresses aspects of your personal learning journey and guides you to use the directional tools appropriately in your life.

All chapters include a review of the chapter's key ideas called, **Boxing the Compass**, followed by **Taking Stock** activities intended to extend the "aha moments" that have occurred as you interacted with the ideas and information contained in the chapter. Finally, at the end of each chapter you will find a practice worksheet, reflective exercise, or Compass Rose figure to complete.

Each of the activities encourages you to implement the insights gained from the chapter. After all, having begun a personal learning journey that results in significant learning outcomes, why would you not want to share the defining experience with others who are part of your varied learning environments?

Finding Your Way: Navigating Your Future by Understanding Your Learning Self provides you with a unique opportunity to affirm yourself as a learner, regardless of your age or stage in life. Most important, it guides your journey to achieve success in the myriad of life's central issues: school, career, relationships, and work. Read these pages thoughtfully, do the suggested activities, and allow yourself to grow in your ability to make your learning journey even more fulfilling.

Finding Your Way:
Setting the Course

I. EXAMINING
THE COORDINATES IN YOUR LIFE

*"It is a sad fate for a man to die
too well known to everybody else,
and still unknown to himself."*
—Sir Francis Bacon

The Focus

- *Examining your personal True North*
- *Understanding yourself as a college learner*

You may not have recognized it, but the reality is when you entered college you began a journey of exploration. That's right. More than being a student, you became an explorer. Like the ancient mariners, your college years are a time to explore the opportunities the future holds for you. Early on you may have been certain of your destination and may have charted your course to achieve your graduation goal. This is the status of approximately 25% of all college students. For the other three-quarters, having a set destination is not as clear. Even for those who thought they knew where they were heading, once in college they may face the reality that thinking about a career and actually living the career day-in-and-day-out are not the same. And for still others, life can intervene and disrupt even the most well planned journey.

I think the college years find most students coping with what I refer to as the Columbus syndrome:

- affirming the known;
- facing the unknown;
- exploring;
- landing where you didn't expect;
- rethinking your destination;
- charting a new course; and finally
- sighting and finding safe harbor.

The challenge college poses for students is not for the faint hearted-well over 50% exit without completing their degree. The reasons can be boiled down to two factors: students who successfully complete college and find meaningful employment have 1) a deep and abiding sense of purpose (owning their True North) and 2) an awareness of who they are as learners, and how to use that knowledge with intention to embrace life's opportunities and confront life's challenges.

> *Students who successfully complete college and find meaningful employment have 1) a deep and abiding sense of purpose (owning their True North) and 2) an awareness of who they are as learners, and how to use that knowledge with intention to embrace life's opportunities and confront life's challenges.*

True North

It isn't easy to navigate among the choices that lie ahead for you. The first and sometimes the biggest challenge is to identify your True North (a nautical term). While ancient astronomers and mariners used to stare at the night sky and glory in its magnitude and beauty, the night sky served a vital purpose for them: It was the only means for finding their way. Until the development of more modern technology, the North Star and Southern Cross (pole stars in the Northern and Southern Hemispheres respectively), were the central reference points for all navigation. However interesting the nautical term is, even more so is its metaphorical application.

> **Within each of us lies our True North.**

Today, we stare at that same night sky and marvel at its beauty, but few of us would see it as a means for finding our way. Yet the evening sky does hold for us a metaphorical significance: Embedded within each of us lies our North Star, our Southern Cross, our figurative reference point that helps us find our way. Just as the mariners of old were carefully schooled in their knowledge of the North Star and the

Southern Cross, this chapter encourages you to study your personal universe, identifying the Polaris or the purpose of your life. After all, if you are preparing to achieve your life goal, it is important for you to consider what the driving force, the source of your persistence to achieve is (your True North)!

In seeking to identify and articulate your True North, consider each of the following questions:

- What is your abiding passion?
- What drives your sense of self?
- What fuels your effort and drives your sense of being?
- What provides the greatest fulfillment for you?
- What is your purpose in life?

Once identified, this chapter is designed to engage you in identifying how important your True North has been to you and how you have used it throughout your life—even during your childhood. In other words, it asks you to recall what experiences you have had that shaped and molded your perspective on life and resulted in what you have chosen to value as central to your life. After all, your True North is not something you chose randomly, but something that evolved over time as you developed from childhood to adulthood.

Identifying My True North

- Do I have a sense of my life purpose?
- Am I passionate about this purpose?
- Do I value and cherish learning about it?
- Does it truly define me?

The Story

My Learning Journey

I was raised in Northern Wisconsin by parents who adopted me when they were 36 and 41 respectively. These dear people of faith caringly loved and nurtured me but were often bewildered by my behavior and learning habits. My father, an electrical engineer and church musician, dutifully sought to rein in my free spirit whenever he thought I was setting myself up for failure or embarrassment. Meanwhile, my mother, at one time a legal secretary, kept copious journals and ran a very well-organized household. She "schooled" me in how to organize my room, develop a weekly dinner menu, and maintain a house-hold the likes of which the National Homemakers of America would be proud.

Blessedly, my parents appreciated my idea of turning my bed room closet into a newspaper office and author's den. They smiled proudly when I published my first book, consisting of my hand-printed sentences interwoven with pictures cut from Christmas cards and nested in balls of cotton glued on tin foil. They drew the line, however, when at age five, I went out on my first reporting venture, walking the shoulder of a busy US federal highway to find my brother at his grade school almost two miles away! Thankfully, they did not judge me or punish me for the apparent differences we had, but instead they sought to accommodate my unique perspective on learning and living while refining my social graces to fit the more staid, conventional culture in which I was being raised.

I began my formal schooling in a renovated two-room chicken coop. I thrived on listening to the teacher and students of the other three grades who occupied my classroom. I was never bored because there were too many things going on to keep me occupied. I reveled in the myriad of activities I could watch or do on my own. My idea bank grew and grew with every passing week.

After my elementary years, I was sent to a large regional junior-senior high where I soon recognized that "kids from the country" were not expected to excel. But I did. Early on, I staked out where I could succeed (debate and forensics), set goals for what I wanted to achieve during my four years of high school (recognition for a unique accomplishment), and began to break the mold of others' expectations of me. By this time, you may have surmised that breaking the mold by bringing unique ideas to the table appears to be the repeated theme of my learning journey, and it is. But often, my ideas were not well received.

> *...breaking the mold by bringing unique ideas to the table appears to be the repeated theme of my learning journey...*

For example, I had a geometry teacher who was new to teaching. He was determined to do what most first-year teachers do—get a handle on classroom management. Unfortunately, he went a bit overboard. He required that if we arrived late to class for any reason, we were to stand the remainder of the class period at our desk. I convinced my fellow college-prep classmates to "boycott the bell" by standing outside the door until the period bell had rung and then enter the classroom. We then stood as a group for the next 55 minutes. The young geometry teacher, who was short of stature, soon found himself staring up at his students! He realized that his rule had created more problems than solutions for him, and he grudgingly discontinued the rule, but not without first noting who had led the insurrection.

When I entered college, I brought my breaking-the-mold learning behaviors with me. In Comp I class, I simply took each assignment as described in the syllabus, twisted it until I was comfortable with it, and then wrote what I wanted to write. I had no idea how to "decode" the meaning of the writing assignment. I had no idea where the professor was coming from and that what was assigned was done with a specific intent. I didn't see the plan, the purpose of it. Besides, I thought I had a better idea for the assignment. So off I went, breaking the mold of the syllabus to create a match between how I learned and the task at hand.

I graduated from college three years to the day I graduated from high school. I had learned lots of "stuff" but nothing that would help me navigate life. Looking back, I recognize now what I did not understand then: I let ideas rule my life. *Different, scattered, mentally playful, full of risk taking, unbounded*—that is who I was, and to a great degree, still am. These behaviors manifested themselves in my life throughout school, college, and my several careers in planning, teaching, and consulting.

For many years, I was not able to understand why I did what I did or saw the world as I did. I was simply aware that as a student, teacher, trainer, urban planner, union organizer, curriculum coordinator, consultant, and professor, I walked, hopped, and danced to the proverbial sound of a different drummer! Thankfully my learning journey did not end at that point.

The Learning

It took me 20 years, two more degrees, and four professions to recognize that I could unravel the enigma I was to myself and others. The insights that helped me direct my actions to achieve my True North were slow in coming. I fought the need to slow down and dig deeply. (I completed my master's degree in urban planning in 15 months and my doctorate in educational leadership in three years.) I needed to consider what it is about a rule that raises my ire and what it is about ideas that lights my fire! Painfully, I had to confront the fact that getting a high from ideas or always seeking the fastest way to get things done had cheated me out of a true sense of myself and my capacity. It limited my potential to become what I set out to be in life: an effective teacher of others.

It has only been over the past third of my life that I have come to grips with the fact that my learning behaviors are identical to my teaching and leading behaviors. I taught content, initiated programs, and took on new ventures without ever understanding what was directing me. I never invested in understanding how to bring others along with my thinking and my ways of doing things. I was not helping others learn what I was trying to teach them. I was imposing on them my way of "taking in the world around me and making sense of it" (a definition I coined fifteen years ago, to describe learning in the context of the real world, not the classroom). I did so without equipping them to digest what I was feeding them. I didn't recognize I was teaching in a manner that worked for me but not for them.

A review of my journey brought me to the stark realization that while I was leading some students, I was ignoring and denying others. Those who learned as I did, felt successful and rewarded under my tutelage and leadership, while those who learned differently were undernourished or confused. They felt left behind in the dust of "hurry up," "please me," "take risks," "quit asking so many questions," and "just take assignment and do it however you can make it work."

In other words, I was not helping them to *find their way*. I was not helping them to understand their learning selves. I was not coaching them to examine their experiences and to see the consistency or inconsistency of their choices. I was not helping them find a sense of their True North or directing their actions to achieve it. Because I did not take the time to reflect on my own way of learning, I actually impeded their ability to find their way by not encouraging them to reflect on their learning experiences.

Your Learning Journey:

Many students believe that the college experience simply involves learning more information, only at a faster speed or a higher level of understanding than when in high school. *Few recognize that the key to successful college level performance is to know how you learn.* They believe that college will be similar to their earlier classroom experiences: the teacher tells the student information; and the student, in turn, records the information, and regurgitates it on demand. Not only is this an inaccurate and very limited description of learning, but it is not at all in keeping with what the 21st century college graduate will be expected to do.

> *The key to success in college is knowing how you learn.*

A more accurate definition of learning that represents the college experience is the following: "Learning involves taking in the world around you, making sense of it, and developing the knowledge and skills to respond appropriately" (Johnston, 2001). In other words, understanding how you, as an individual, "take in the world around you and make sense of it," is the single most important factor determining your success in college and your success within your chosen career. The college experience is about learning how to learn so that you can 1) take that understanding of how your mind works into any workplace, career, professional training, or team situation; and 2) conduct yourself as a competent and capable adult. More than maps and sextants, more than high-tech gadgets, more than an understanding of the laws of physics, we need an understanding of how we learn and the knowledge of how to apply it to achieve our life potential.

We are not the first people who have sought the best means for finding our way. I am certain that it has been true throughout history: Men and women have striven to achieve their utmost potential. What tools have they have used to achieve this success? I would suggest it is their Learning Processes—their Patterned Operations used in concert with their innate human abilities. It is the joining of our intellectual potential, in its multiple forms, with our Patterned operations that equips us to take in the world around us and make sense of it. Women, men, and children all possess these Processes and hold the potential to use them to make their lives work.

But how well do they use them? How well do you use your Learning Processes? How prepared are you to set your life course by using your learning tools? How prepared are you to adapt, overcome, and succeed?

My Learning Journey Revisited

Looking back at my life, I recognize that my learning journey often was at odds with the learning situations in which I found myself. I was the one whose ideas were askew or inconsistent with those of the people around me at home, in school, or at work. Underlying it all was the fact that I never felt valued or accepted for who I was.

Because I felt that I was a bit of an outsider, I was always empathetic with those who found themselves not fitting in, whether in the classroom or in the workplace. I cared about what they were experiencing, and I wanted them to feel valued. It has only been in the last twenty years that have I discovered how to help them—and myself. After several decades, I have found a sense of fulfillment as I continue on my personal learning journey. This sense comes from having identified my True North, *my purpose in life—to help people whose sense of self as learners is unrecognized, undervalued, or underused.*

This book is an extension of my True North as I seek to share with you how you too can find your way and gain an awareness of your purpose by exploring your learning journey. If it achieves its purpose, it will help you recognize your True North, identify the power of your Learning Processes, and apply that knowledge to achieve safe harbor, having achieved the desires of your heart.

Boxing the Compass

- Recognizing the central role of your personal learning story helps you identify your True North and set the course for navigating your life.
- Understanding the importance of your personal Learning Processes is central to all of your life's journey.

Taking Stock

1) Map your learning journey.

- Think about your learning journey.
- If you had to chart your journey, what would your map look like?
- Where were the critical stopping points?
- Where were the high and low points in the journey?
- List the five most important stops you have made along your life journey.
- If you had to create a road sign for each stop, what would it look like?
- How do these signs relate to your True North?

Reflect on These Success Factors

Factors Influencing My Success in Achieving a Degree	My Answer Use a question mark (?) if you're unsure.
Motivation: What motivates me most to complete a college degree?	
Purpose: How will a college degree help me achieve employment?	
Values: What *values* am I demonstrating by seeking my college degree?	
Discipline: How willing am I to *schedule* my life to include time for career preparation and pursuit of employment?	
Focus: What will I say to myself that will help me persist and persevere when I feel overwhelmed by work? Family? Other *responsibilities?*	

Worksheet 1.1: Reflect on These Success Factors

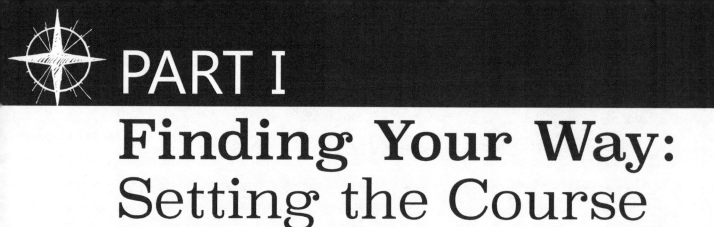

PART I
Finding Your Way:
Setting the Course

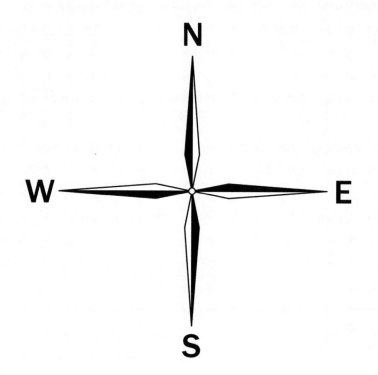

II. UNDERSTANDING WHAT
COMPRISES YOUR COMPASS ROSE

*"Taking charge of your own learning
is part of taking charge of your own life."*
—Warren Bennis
On Becoming a Leader

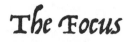

The Focus

• *Understanding the concept of the Compass Rose*
• *Identifying the directional tools of the mind*

You may be familiar with the design of a Compass Rose because you have seen it on a road map, as a piece of jewelry, or possibly even as a tattoo. However, none of these forms explains the important role the Compass Rose has played over the course of navigation history. Its purpose was to help navigators identify and harness the various directional winds (32 in number) available to propel their ships to reach a specific destination.

Today's maps bear little resemblance to the intricacy and beauty of a cartographer's rendering of a Compass Rose. However, while more sophisticated navigational technology long ago replaced the Compass Rose, the image of it still speaks to us today as a robust metaphorical image, reminding us of our need to have sound navigational tools to use in our everyday lives. After all, citizens of the 21st century continue to be confronted by the age-old need to *find their way in life*. And while navigational technology has leaped light years ahead, the challenge of knowing one's True North and the means by which to achieve one's life goals remains fundamentally the same.

We each can benefit from having a personal Compass Rose helping us navigate our learning lives cognizant of our True North. And just as the young sailors of ancient times needed to determine and understand the effects of the 32 winds of the compass rose to successfully navigate the seas, so too do we need to be able to name and understand the Directional Forces within each of us.

What is it that each of us possesses that forms our personal Compass Rose? What is it about our mental processes that serve as our Compass Rose of Directional Forces? What determines our direction? Albert Einstein suggested it stems from our human curiosity that can be described as the awareness that "there must be something deeply hidden behind everything" (Schilpp, 1979; Davies, 2007; Dyson, 2007). Einstein wrote of this experience:

> *I think that wondering to one's self occurs when an experience conflicts with our fixed ways of seeing the world. I had one such experience of wondering when I was a child of four or five and my father showed me a compass. This needle behaved in such a determined way and did not fit into the usual explanation of how the world works. (That is that you must touch something to move it.) I still remember now, or I believe that I remember, that this experience made a deep and lasting impression on me. There must be some thing deeply hidden behind everything (Schilpp p. 9).*

I would suggest that each of us has a Compass Rose of Directional Forces that lies deeply hidden in our brain-mind connection and drives our approach to learning. These directions for learning form our internal compass. If we allow our Directional Forces to remain undiscovered and unfettered, then we travel at their behest, buffeted from one position to another, one career to another, one relationship to another, without ever determining our current position or plotting a way to reach our destination.

If we allow our Directional Forces to remain undiscovered and unfettered, then we travel at their behest, buffeted from one position to another, one career to another, one relationship to another, without ever determining our current position or plotting a way to reach our destination.

To understand our learning selves is to set ourselves on a course of self-awareness and preparedness as no other single piece of knowledge can. In Chapter I, we identified the centrality of our True North to the course of our lives. This chapter continues that message, pointing out that each of us must grab hold of our Directional Forces (Learning Processes) and understand the directional tool they can be for achieving our True North.

The Story

John Harrison was an 18th Century inventor of the chronometer, the first reliable means for navigators to measure longitude. He was a brilliant scientist, but he lacked an understanding of himself as a learner and how uniquely he took in the world around him and made sense of it. Harrison worked well with his hands. He understood a great deal about how the world operated, but he lacked the use of words to express what he could see in his mind and engineer with his genius. (Sobel, 1996; Macaulay,1836).

As a result, Harrison struggled for 16 years to earn, what in today's currency, would amount to a million dollar award by explaining his invention in writing to the British Royale Observatory. In the initial paper he submitted along with a model of his invention, he used a sentence that went on for five pages with no punctuation! The paper jumped from one idea to another, never completing one point before moving on to another. The Royal Observatory declared him an "idiot" and sent his rival to bring Harrison's invention to their location. In an unseemly set of events, the rival dropped Harrison's invention down a flight of stairs, destroying it. The Royal Society then suggested that if he (Harrison) truly had developed the intricate tool for measuring longitude, he could certainly re-build it as proof of his inventiveness. Harrison thus labored 16 more years before he submitted another version of the original chronometer, along with a paper explaining the science behind it. Finally, after 32 years, he could claim the million dollar reward offered by the Royale Society for solving the problem of how to measure longitude at sea!

Tragically for Harrison, he didn't understand that his tools for learning consisted primarily of his hands and his ability to think without words. Consequently, when he went to explain his invention, he lacked the skill to organize and communicate his thoughts in an efficient and effective manner. Had John Harrison been aware of how he learned and had he been aware that his approach to learning was different from those to whom he was presenting his invention, he could have consciously chosen to refine and retool his approach so that he could have achieved his life goal much earlier and with much less frustration.

There is no doubt that John Harrison was a great man of science, but he lacked an understanding of himself as a learner and therefore, struggled to respond appropriately to others who took in the world around him differently. Clearly he engaged in the first two aspects of learning: 1) Taking in the world around him; and 2) Making sense of it. However, he failed to understand the third aspect of learning, 3) "responding appropriately."

Just imagine the pain and frustration he experienced throughout his life because of his lack of awareness of his internal Compass Rose of Learning Processes. To revisit Einstein's comment, "Deeply hidden behind everything" lay the fact that Harrison's mind operated with such precision and detail that he was unable to organize, edit, and articulate his thoughts in a manner that was lucid and comprehensible to others.

The totality of his scientific writings suffered from the same problem. In 1775, when he was 82, he wrote an account of his life's work. He entitled his book, *A Description Concerning Such Mechanism As Will Afford a Nice, or True Mensuration of Time; Together With Some Account of the Attempts for the Discovery of the Longitude by the Moon: As Also An Account of the Discovery of the Scale of Music, by John Harrison, Inventor of the Time-Keeper For The Longitude At Sea.* John Harrison, unaware of his internal Compass Rose of Learning Processes, became the victim of them. Herein lies the irony!

Of what did John Harrison's Compass Rose of Learning Processes consist? They were made up of four distinct processes: his Sequence or ability to follow directions and complete tasks in a timely and organized manner; his Precision or his use of details, facts, and words; his Technical Reasoning or ability to problem solve and carefully puzzle over challenging aspects of how the world works; and finally his Confluence or willingness to take risks and try new things.

Pattern	Responsible for
Sequence	Order, planning, organization
Precision	Accuracy, detail, and information
Technical Reasoning	Problem solving, relevance, and autonomy
Confluence	Ideas, uniqueness, and risk taking

Table 2.1: The Four Learning Patterns

Put in this context of Directional Forces, it becomes clearer that Harrison's True North lay in his determination to solve a problem whose solution evaded the most erudite minds of his time. His learning processes consisted of his powers of observation (Precision), his doggedness to find solutions (Technical Reasoning), and his workmanship (Precision and Technical Reasoning). Yet Harrison's Compass Rose of Learning tools, the very thing that powered his genius, provided him with years of frustration, and left him diminished in spirit and professional stature.

Harrison, who worked his entire life to solve the most challenging problem of sea navigation, landed personally on the rocky shoals of failed communication, preventing him from achieving, in his lifetime, the prominence and success he was rightfully due. Years later, the British historian Thomas Babington Macaulay would describe him as, "a great man with the wisdom to devise and the courage to perform that which he lacked the language to explain" (Smiles, 1884).

The Learning

When we can identify the Learning Processes that comprise our Compass Rose, we can use our Directional Forces to navigate our lives so that we can "respond appropriately" to the tasks and challenges set before us, and we can succeed. Maybe you are seeking the essence of your True North. Is it found in entrepreneurship, teaching others, the high tech industry, medicine, science, technology, engineering, the arts, mathematics (STEAM) social services, business or finance? How will you know if your Compass Rose consists of the mental processes needed to achieve your True North? Maybe your situation is much like that of someone I know.

Gregory's Journey (Dr. Gregory Dunham)

Gregory is a high school principal who was raised in the Boston area. Greg's mother nurtured his interest in academics and kept a tight rein on him until he completed high school and entered college, where he majored in engineering. His school counselor suggested he do so because of Greg's mathematical abilities. Four years later, he found himself employed as an engineer but very unhappy. Clearly it wasn't his True North.

He wrote:

I actually began my professional life as a research and development engineer for a transistor company that grew silicone chips for use in miniature amplifiers. I enjoyed the prestige of my career but soon began to feel isolated, having no meaningful interaction with people during my working hours. My fondest memories of that company were during lunch, when the entire research unit ate together, and we told stories and shared experiences.

After a while, I began to wonder why and how I chose engineering as my career. I reflected on my high school days. I was always a very good math student, and one day my guidance counselor asked, "Gregory, what do you want to do when you graduate from high school?" I had no idea.

She said, "You know, with your math aptitude you could be an engineer." It sounded good to me. When I told my parents that I wanted to be an engineer, they were pleased. When I told my friends that I was going to be an engineer, they were impressed.

The interesting thing about that decision is that it was totally based on one aspect of what I did well, but it did not take into consideration my passion, my True North. Within a few years, I changed careers and took my math skills into secondary education, and I became a high school math teacher.

It was not until many years later, having achieved the position of high school principal, that I became aware of how it was possible to have been so mismatched with my first career: My high school counselor had no real basis on which to help me select an appropriate career because she had no idea who I was beyond my record of grades and activities.

Later in life when I finally learned about my Learning Processes, my awareness of what went wrong back then was truly cathartic for me. For years, I wondered why I did not find engineering energizing, but I loved teaching math. As I spent time looking back on my learning journey, examining it vis-á-vis my knowledge of my learning self, it became very clear: I was good in math because I had an innate mathematical intelligence, which I processed by asking questions until I understood. I also learned by being allowed to see things in more than one way and being able to take some risks. This helped me particularly with geometry. Yet I still needed to understand why engineering was not energizing to me, a person who had a strong math aptitude. I found the explanation by examining my Learning Processes— my Compass Rose. I did not find fulfillment in an engineering career because I did not have a natural curiosity about how things worked. I lacked technical curiosity.

If my guidance counselor had known my Learning Processes, she could have made more informed recommendations to me regarding my future. More important, if I had knowledge of the Learning Forces that made up my Compass Rose, I could have had more control over my choices and could have made them with more intention.

> *...if I had knowledge of the Learning Forces that made up my Compass Rose, I could have had more control over my choices and could have made them with more intention.*

Three careers and many years later, Dr. Gregory Dunham finally found his way. Like Gregory, unless you understand the composition of your internal Compass Rose, you will survive by chance, not succeed and achieve through conscious planning and focused effort.

The Price of Being Compass-Less

Just like John Harrison and Gregory Dunham, millions of people possess the innate ability and talent to succeed, but they do not know how to use their Directional Forces to achieve fulfillment. Many go through life with an intuitive sense of their Compass Rose, but fail to use their internal Directional Learning Forces to achieve their desired outcomes.

Think of the consequences of not knowing your True North or not being able to explain the combination of your Learning Processes. Consider the limitations of a college advisor or career counselor who seeks to provide direction to others without knowledge of their advisees' Compass Rose of Learning Processes? Or think about the positive effect understanding your instructor's Learning Processes can have on your ability to follow his/her syllabus? Directions? Grading rubric?

Think about the future benefits of being able to bring the understanding of your Directional Forces into the work place. What happens if you are promoted to a position that has been your lifelong dream, and suddenly, all of the means you used to achieve this success are no longer working for you? You find yourself sailing different seas with no Directional Forces to guide you. Did your True North change? Did you leave your Compass Rose behind? Did you find that the things you used intuitively before are not working effectively anymore? That's when it dawns on you: In making the change in career positions you failed to consider how the new position would impact your Directional Forces. It isn't long before you realize that revisiting the composition of your Compass Rose and using its Directional Forces is key to adjusting to the new demands of your work life. Knowledge of your Directional Forces is required every day for every aspect of your life.

Knowledge of your Directional Forces is required every day for every aspect of your life.

Finding Your Way: Identifying Your Compass Rose

Identifying your Compass Rose begins by collecting data about yourself—how you think, what actions you take as a result, and what your emotions respond to in different situations. Twenty years ago, my graduate assistant and I developed a means to gather that information and interpret it in a valid and reliable manner. You can find a version of that instrument, the **Learning Connections Inventory**® (LCI), in Appendix A. Using the directions provided under Taking Stock, at the conclusion of this chapter, complete the survey and gain a more complete representation of the Compass Rose of your Learning Processes.©

Here is an opportunity to develop an awareness of your personal Compass Rose using the information gathered by completing the LCI. The development of your personal Compass Rose marks the beginning of a new venture in *finding your way.*

Boxing the Compass

- Learning Processes provide a powerful insight into your communication with others as well as an understanding of yourself. There's little use having a True North if you don't have the navigational tools to help you reach your destination.
- Understanding the direction of your Learning Processes provides a powerful insight into your communication with others as well as an understanding of yourself.

Taking Stock

1) Complete the Learning Connections Inventory (See Appendix A or complete online via your university's license.). This is a survey that identifies the degree to which you use each of your individual Learning Processes. This is the first step in developing your Compass Rose of Learning Processes:

- Before you begin Part I, take a moment to write your definition for each of the choices you have on the continuum. Think and determine what is an "Always" for you? A "Never?" An "Almost Always" (daily with few exceptions)? An "Almost Never" (once or twice a year)?"
- Note that you are free to tweak a word or phrase within a given question if you feel changing the wording will help you respond with a more accurate choice on the continuum.
- Avoid using "Sometimes" as your answer unless the answer truly is sometimes. Don't use "Sometimes" as your answer when you can't decide what the answer should be. Instead, stop and think. Is this something I do a few times a month, for instance? Is "occasionally" a word that I think of as "sometimes?"
- Now begin Part I, answering questions 1 through 28.
- Remember, you are the expert when it comes to answering the questions.
- After completing Part I, complete Part II by responding to the three open-ended questions. Do not skip this portion of the survey, as your answers to the questions are key to being able to score and validate your outcome.
- Take your time and enjoy doing both parts of the survey!

2) Score your LCI responses:
- When you have finished answering Parts I and II, read the directions for scoring the LCI which are printed at the top of the scoring sheet. Once you have completed transferring your answers from Part I to the scoring sheet, add up your scores for each category, and fill in the graph at the bottom of the score sheet (See Figure A.2.1 Scoring Sheet).
- Take note of the degree to which you use each of your Learning Processes. Which of these Directional Forces do you Use First, Use as Needed, and Avoid?
- Whenever someone completes the LCI it is very important that the outcome be validated. Validation means that a check is made to see if the outcome is reasonable. To do that see if the scores match what you wrote as your short answers. This internal validity check helps strengthen your reliance on the learning profile revealed by the LCI. (See Figure A. 2.2 Comparison of Scores to Short Answers).
- After scoring your LCI and filling in the graph, return to this page.

3) Now enter your LCI Scores in the compass rose below. Note the designation for where to place each being careful to match the scores with the correct Directional Force located on the blank Compass Rose.

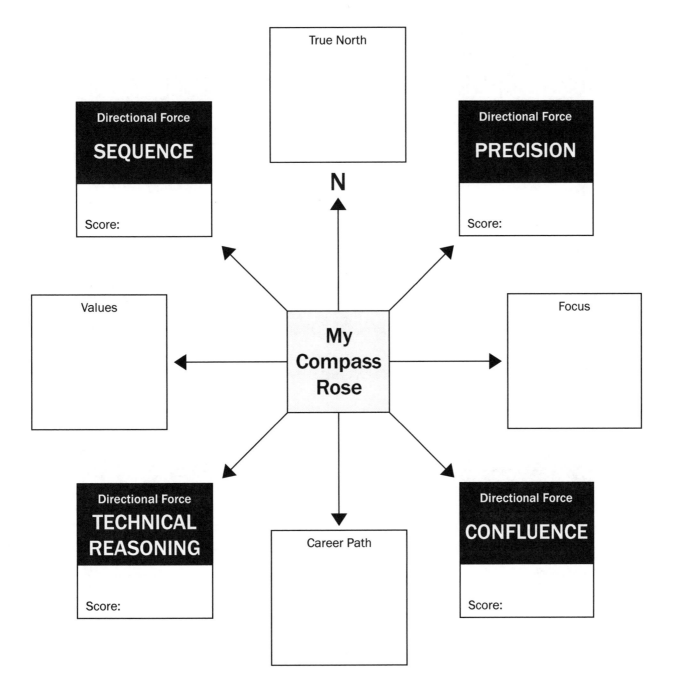

True North

Directional Force

SEQUENCE

Score:

Directional Force

PRECISION

Score:

N

Values

My Compass Rose

Focus

Directional Force

TECHNICAL REASONING

Score:

Career Path

Directional Force

CONFLUENCE

Score:

Worksheet 2.1: Blank: My Compass Rose

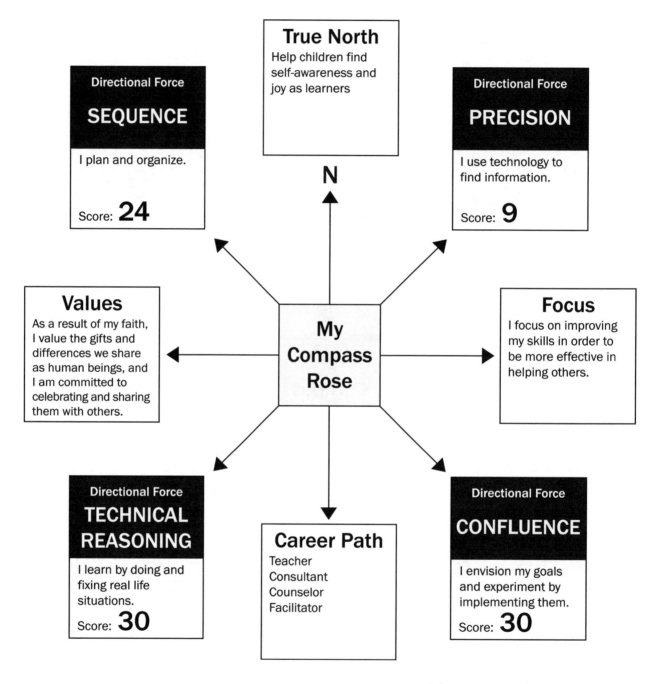

True North

Help children find self-awareness and joy as learners

Directional Force

SEQUENCE

I plan and organize.

Score: **24**

Directional Force

PRECISION

I use technology to find information.

Score: **9**

N

Values

As a result of my faith, I value the gifts and differences we share as human beings, and I am committed to celebrating and sharing them with others.

My Compass Rose

Focus

I focus on improving my skills in order to be more effective in helping others.

Directional Force

TECHNICAL REASONING

I learn by doing and fixing real life situations.

Score: **30**

Career Path

Teacher
Consultant
Counselor
Facilitator

Directional Force

CONFLUENCE

I envision my goals and experiment by implementing them.

Score: **30**

Worksheet 2.2: Example: My Compass Rose

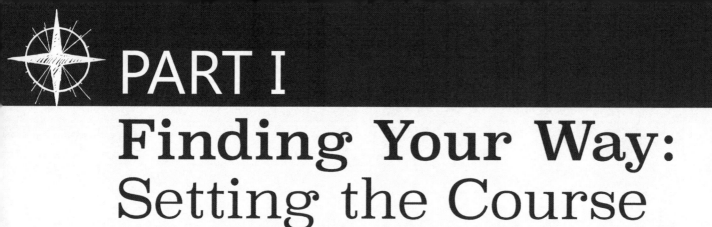

PART I
Finding Your Way:
Setting the Course

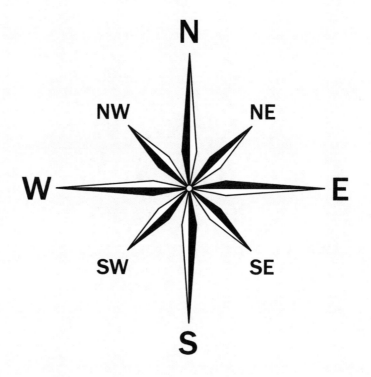

III. CONFIGURING YOUR COMPASS ROSE

*"Real learning gets to the heart
of what it means to be human."*
—Peter Senge
The Fifth Discipline

The Focus

- *Understanding our internal Directional Forces (Learning Processes)*
- *Understanding how these forces affect how we navigate life*

The first two chapters of this text have had you explore your previous learning experiences, identify your True North, and reflect on the role learning plays in helping you find your way and navigate life. This chapter now takes you deeper into understanding your learning self (the second part of the book's title) by revealing to you how the act of learning works within you specifically. I have long said that learning is the most personal—universal aspect of our human existence. Everybody learns. Everybody! But everybody does not learn in the same way. This chapter will help you understand the configuration of your learning forces and in the chapters that follow how you can use this enhanced understanding of yourself to *navigate life.*

Learning is the center of our human essence. Learning directs our thoughts, our actions, and our feelings. It gives us a sense of being; it enables us to function, to grow in understanding, and to change because we have chosen to do so. The act of learning is made possible because we are physically equipped to take in the world around us through the use of our senses. Our senses (sight, sound, touch, taste, and smell) send stimuli from the external world into our brain where it is processed, then filtered by our brain-mind interface, and handed over to our mind where it is translated, stored, and used to make life work for us.

Most of this explanation is commonly known. However, what is less known is the role our Learning Processes (Directional Forces) play as we take in the world around us. It is our Learning Processes that act as filters between our brain and mind determining the degree and pace at which various stimuli enter our mind. It is our Learning Processes that form the Directional Forces of our individual Compass Roses.

As a result of the role our Directional Forces play in our learning, we need to become very familiar with how they contribute to what we experience as learners. Clearly, if we intend to navigate our lives well, if we intend to "set our course, stay the course, and come safe home," then we need to know how to use our Directional Learning Forces to achieve that destination. Beyond any doubt, understanding our Learning Processes is the first step to finding our way in the world of learning.

The Story

The Brain-Mind Connection

Earlier, I referred to learning as interacting with the world around us. Learning requires our brain to connect and respond to sensory stimuli, but learning also involves the mind—which is more than the machinery that sits atop our shoulders. Our minds go far beyond the physiological limitations of our gray matter. In this chapter The Story focuses not on a single human being, but instead focuses on each of us and how we make the very heart of who we are—how we learn—understandable to ourselves and others.

Our story of learning begins long before we embark on formal schooling. It starts as our senses, our brain, and our mind form an intricate system by which we take in the world around us and make sense of it. What follows is a simple representation of that extremely complex operation. Read the explanation of this system, better known as the brain-mind connection, for the insight and understanding it provides, not as a detailed science text. (See Figure 3.2.)

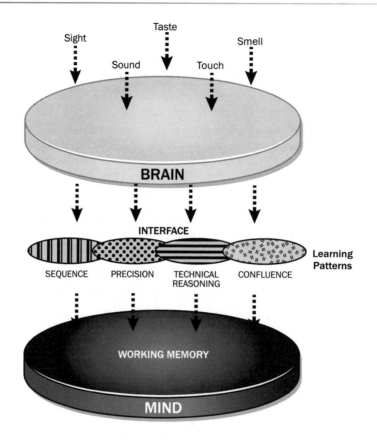

Figure 3.2: Understanding the function of the brain-mind interface increases learners' ability to take control of their learning.

Learning—it all begins with our senses. Our ears, eyes, nose, skin, and tongue serve as the first line receptors that initiate learning. They gather and channel stimuli into the brain, which sends it through its complex circuitry of neurons. No doubt about it, Einstein was correct when he referred to the mind as the greatest complexity in the universe. In the brain's electrochemical processing, the stimuli are "handled" by a number of operations, and ultimately enter into our mental processing (the mind). (Johnston, 1994; Bruer, 1997). During the stimuli's passage between the brain and the mind it is filtered by our individual Learning Processes and either blocked, welcomed, or given limited access to operate within our minds.

I believe that our Compass Rose of Learning lies (figuratively) at the juncture where our sensory stimuli morph from electrochemical impulses into symbolic representation (oral and written language, numbers, musical notes, etc.).The stimuli that make it through the brain-mind interface enter the mind and are translated into symbols and passed to either our working memory to become a part of our consciousness (declarative or factual memory) or to our sub consciousness (non-declarative memory) where they shape our values, and beliefs, effect our sense of self, and form our associative memory and also our muscle memory.

The degree to which you use each Learning Process is measured by how it limits or grants the stimuli access to the mind's working memory. Think of the four Learning Processes as filters with varying densities through which stimuli flow. For example, a broad mesh filter (Use First) allows large amounts of stimuli to pass into the working memory for translation and storage. Conversely, a tightly woven filter

(Avoid) may severely limit stimuli from passing through the brain-mind interface to the working memory. The Use As Needed configuration of a Process allows a steady but somewhat limited flow of stimuli to pass through it.

Within each of these filtering processes are the mental processes of **cognition (thoughts), conation (actions),** and **affectation (feelings).** It is the interplay among your thoughts, actions, and feelings (see Figure 3.3) that creates a sense of comfort and wellbeing or discomfort and frustration within each and among the four Learning Processes (MacLean, 1978).

It is the mental processes **(thoughts, actions, feelings)** within each Learning Process or Directional Force that personalizes the act of learning in each of us.

Figure 3.3: Each of the Learning Patterns contains the mental processes of cognition (thoughts), conation (actions), and affection (feelings.)

The Learning

The Compass Rose of Our Learning

Our Compass Rose of Learning represents the manner in which each of us learns. Unlike our genetically endowed traits of multiple intelligences and personality, the way we learn is the result of our brain and mind as they seek unity and wholeness. As Sherwin Nuland (2007) of Yale said, our brain-mind connection forms "a rhythm and harmony of operation, selecting the cells it values, favoring those that create a unity, and shunning those that give a sense of chaos."

As we reflect on the Directional Forces of our Compass Rose (i.e., the Learning Processes that operate in our minds), we recognize that these processes play a key role in our internal learning system. To put this very important information into a more concrete context, consider the following examples of how our Learning Processes manifest themselves in daily life.

Scenario 1

You sit in class using your laptop to record copious notes. You look around you and wonder, "Why is Gina studying the syllabus so closely instead of recording what is being said? And what is Sam doing checking Facebook on his cell? Grow up and pay attention, fella! Does he think he can memorize all this? And then there's Celine. I swear if she interrupts the flow of the presentation one more time with her 'alternative' idea, I'm going to scream. What is it with this class? It's obvious no one will know anything about what is being said when the class is over—except me, of course, because I took notes. But then again, if I didn't have my fingers recording what was happening, I'd feel like a fish out of water."

Scenario 2

Three people, standing in the same location, observe a car accident, a minor fender-bender. Each is asked to tell what he or she saw:

Person A says:

I was standing approximately 20-feet away, waiting for the 7:35 bus to take me uptown. I know what time it was because I had just looked at my watch and was wondering why the bus was running late. Then this late-model, blue Chevy just came out of nowhere and broadsided the tan Camry that was waiting to turn left on the arrow. The young man in the Chevy—I'd guess no more than 20 years of age and similar to my son in height and weight who just turned 20 last week—jumped out of his car and began to yell, "Look what you've done now!" at the young mother. Well I assume she was a mother because she had a crumpled child safety seat in her backseat—thank heavens there wasn't a child in it.

Person B reports:

First, this car came up really fast, then it tried to brake but couldn't, so it skidded and slammed into the other car that was in the left turn lane. I looked to see if anyone was hurt. The next thing I knew, a fellow from the first car was yelling, and a woman from the car that was hit was crying. Shortly after that, you folks arrived. Since you are on the scene now, can I leave so I won't be late for work?

Person C relates:

The one car rear-ended the other. Happens all the time at this intersection. No big deal. Can I go now?

Scenario 3

Your parents just saw your second semester grades. Admittedly your grades weren't the best. Now your parents call because they want to know, "What's going on? You did okay (one B and a few C's) in your first semester." Of course your sister nailed all her graduate courses this past semester.

Your parents reinforce that you come from a real good gene pool. You pick up on things quickly. You excel at building things and can figure out the most complex stuff. They want to know why you haven't talked to them about what's happening. ("Well, you're thinking," 'I don't talk a lot about myself to anyone.') They say you've always been a bit lazy. (Frankly, you feel bored.) They sound angry. They want you to get a tutor and make their tuition investment in you worth it.

The previous scenarios undergird the point that we each take in the world around us differently. We process the same stimuli, but to different degrees and from different perspectives. We cannot escape the fact that how we take in the world around us and deal with it, affects our everyday decisions, behaviors, plans—our lives! This book is about taking control of how you learn, and making it work for you so that you can navigate your daily life, as well as your future.

Taking control of your learning begins with an awareness of yourself. In other words, your journey begins by understanding your Compass Rose of Directional Forces or Learning Processes and the effect of their action upon each other.

The Directional Forces of Your Compass Rose: Your Learning Processes

At the conclusion of the previous chapter, you were encouraged to respond to a set of 28 statements as well as record your answers to three open-ended questions. You then tallied your Learning Connections Inventory (LCI) responses and recorded your results in the outline of the Compass Rose provided. The numbers you recorded under each of four categories (Sequence, Precision, Technical Reasoning, and Confluence) identify the degree to which you use each of four Learning Processes or Directional Learning Forces in your life. They form the port of entry to your mind. They represent the organization, information, problem-solving, and risk-taking thoughts, actions, and feelings that help you navigate life. As in the case of the Compass Rose, your Patterns form a set of winds of various strengths coming from various directions.

In this and the ensuing chapters, you will find an explanation of what your Learning Connection Inventory (LCI) scores mean. You will also find ways to use your Directional Learning Forces to navigate your life. If you read this chapter carefully and study its illustrations, you will begin to find your way in a manner you never before experienced.

Your LCI Scale Scores

Your Compass Rose of personal learning forces is comprised of your four Learning Patterns. This portion of the chapter will introduce you to the Patterns and the internal composition of each (MacLean, 1978; Snow, 1997). Like the Compass Rose of old, which was comprised of 32 distinct winds, your Compass Rose is comprised of four Directional Learning Forces and their subsets. Read the following pages with care, noting which aspects of the four Learning Processes form your Compass Rose.

The four Directional Forces of your Compass Rose consist of the four scores recorded on your LCI. (See Figure 3.4 Learning Connections Inventory Scale Scores.) Note that the range of the LCI Scale Scores is 7 through 35. The range of the continuum of the scores form three distinct categories: (1) Use First, (2) Use As Needed, and (3) Avoid.

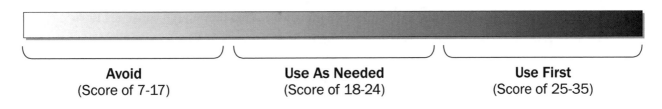

Avoid
(Score of 7-17)

Use As Needed
(Score of 18-24)

Use First
(Score of 25-35)

Figure 3.4: Identifying the range of use of each of your Learning Patterns can provide a valuable insight into who you are as a learner.

Everyone uses each of these Patterns to some degree. The most important aspect of the scores is that they tell you the degree to which you use each Pattern in combination with the others. No single score or group of scores makes you smarter, brighter, more capable, or less capable. Each has equal value when you analyze the totality of the Directional Forces that comprise your Compass Rose of Learning. Even though you have recorded your Scale Scores at the end of the prior chapter, record them again here so you'll have them in front of you to help you recognize what each of your scores signifies:

Sequence _____   Precision_____   Technical Reasoning_____   Confluence_____

Begin the analysis of your Learning Processes by comparing your scores to each of the "degree of use" categories. How many Learning Processes do you use at the Use First level; Use As Needed; how many do you Avoid?

Examining Your Compass Rose

Each Directional Force has specific descriptors as the tables that follow illustrate. Remember, if you use a Learning Pattern in the **Use First range (25 to 35)**, you can expect to find yourself saying yes to most of the Pattern characteristics listed.

The Patterns that fall within the **Use As Needed range (18 to 24)** are the ones that you just don't feel an urgency to use. Sometimes, you actually need to wake them up and let them know that you need to use them—now! If one or more of your Patterns are Use As Needed, you will find yourself saying, "I agree with some of the characteristics and behaviors cited under a specific Pattern category, but not all of them. I don't feel a strong pull to use this Pattern. I can use it when I need to, but it isn't the Directional Force that I am going to use to navigate a learning situation."

If, on the other hand, your score is in the **Avoid range (7 to 17)**, you will find yourself saying, "I truly do not like to use this Pattern. Frankly, I avoid using it whenever I can. I don't understand it. I don't enjoy it, and I simply don't like it."

The Directional Forces of Your Compass Rose: Your Learning Processes

Please note that each set of explanations begins with what **you think, do, feel,** or say if you use the Pattern at the Use First level (LCI Scale Scores 25 to 35) and what you think, do, feel, and say when you truly Avoid the Pattern (LCI Scale Scores 7 to 17). As you read the following descriptions, consider how each pulls you in a different direction, forming the dynamic action of the Directional Forces within you.

Sequence

Sequence is the Learning Process that seeks order and consistency: "I process information step-by-step. I act according to the rules. I want time to present a neat and complete assignment. I may need time to double-check what I have done. Don't rush me, please. Oh, and could I see an example of the final product you expect me to complete?"

SEQUENCE

	Use First	Avoid
What I think	I think in **goals, objectives, steps.** I think with **clarity,** not clutter. I think in phases – **start up, progress, completion.**	These directions are **too wordy and too lengthy!** I **did this before,** why repeat it? **Why must I wait** for directions?
How I act	I break tasks into **steps.** I organize my life by keeping tight **schedules.** I strive to do a **task methodically** from beginning to end.	I **read as little of the directions** as possible. I **don't practice and rehearse.** I **fail to do all the parts of a task** leaving some incomplete.
What I feel	I feel **secure** when I have the **steps laid out.** I **thrive** on a **well-ordered life.** I feel a great sense of **satisfaction when I finish** a task A-Z.	I feel **confused by** the wording and order of most **directions.** I feel **frustrated and bored** when I am forced to **repeat** a task. I **don't** feel **bound by the requirements** of the task.
My internal "chatter"	What's the **goal?** What's the **first step?** There is a **place for everything** and everything in its place. Nothing feels better than **crossing off something on my to-do list.**	**Who wrote** these directions anyway? What a **waste of my time.** **Who cares how I do this** as long as I get it done?

Table 3.1: SEQUENCE

Words that signal Sequence is needed to complete a task or an assignment include: **alphabetize, arrange, classify, compare and contrast, develop, establish an order, evenly distribute, (set) goals, group, list, order, pros and cons, put in a series, put in order, sequence, show an array, show an example.**

Precision

Precision is the Directional Force that wants to know details and exactness: "I process information precisely. I read it carefully; I record it accurately; I store it with specificity; and I respond to it correctly. I feel good about myself as a learner when I get accurate feedback and when I am able to point to specific things I've done that have earned me recognition."

Be careful to distinguish that Precision focuses on the importance of information, accuracy, exactness, and documentation while Sequence refers to order, rules, planning, and completeness. An example of the distinct difference between the two Directional Forces can be observed when a person who uses Precision at the Use First level and Sequence at the Use As Needed level gathers so much information and documentation that his/her office is awash in piles of folders and projects. His combination of Directional Forces does not possess the amount of Sequence needed to be able to organize the amount of information being collected!

PRECISION

	Use First	Avoid
What I think	I think in **information.** I think **knowing facts** means I am smart. I think **knowledge is power.**	How am I **supposed to remember** all this stuff? **Do I have to read all** of this? What am I **expected to write down and keep track of?**
How I act	I **write** things down and **document** everything. I leave no piece **of information** unspoken. I **research information** and **check sources.**	I **don't have specific answers.** I **skim** instead of read details. I **take few, if any, notes.**
What I feel	I feel **confident** when I have **my notes or journal** to refer to. I **hate being "out of the know."** I feel **frustrated when incorrect information** is accepted as valid.	I **feel stupid if I don't have the one expected answer.** Pages of information make me feel like I am **drowning in words.** I **fear looking unprepared** because my **notes are so few.**
My internal "chatter"	Before I decide, I **need more information.** **Where did you get that** information? What was your **source?**	**Stop asking** me so many questions! **Don't expect me to know names and dates!** Do I have to **read all of this?** Is there a DVD I can **watch instead?**

Table 3.2: PRECISION

Words that signal that Precision is needed to complete a task or an assignment include: **calibrate, detail, describe, document, examine, explain, identify, label, measure, name, record (facts), observe, perform accurately, specify**.

It might be tempting to think that those who Avoid Precision cannot do well in the information age, but actually, that is not true. With the availability of information at the touch of search engines (Google, Bing, etc.) research apps, and many other digital sources, those who Avoid Precision can make their world of work operate successfully. What those who Avoid Precision always need to be aware of is not to rely on information sources that would lead them to generalize or rely on abstracts and summaries instead of delving into the body of facts available. Read the descriptors of the Avoid Precision Pattern and determine how to avoid the issues this Pattern may raise for you if you are not alert to its effects on your Compass Rose.

Technical Reasoning

Technical Reasoning, adds an additional component to your Compass Rose. Technical Reasoning processes the world using stand-alone, independent reasoning, and very few words: "Let me figure this out. Let me do this by myself. I see a tool, and I know its use. I'm fascinated by its form and function. I especially like the challenge of using it."

Technical Reasoning's uniqueness (See Table 3.3.) lies in its ability to think and reason without the use of words. It demands relevance and practicality, and confronted with a task, it urges you to "Just do it!" Although Technical Reasoning and Precision can work together at the Use First level, the effect of Technical Reasoning on the flow of information provided by Precision is muted. Only pertinent facts are shared, and "information for information's sake" is not.

Words that signal the Directional Force of Technical Reasoning needed to complete a task or an assignment include the following: **assemble, build, construct, demonstrate, engineer, erect, experience, figure out, fix, implement, "just do it," operate concretely, problem solve, represent graphically**.

TECHNICAL REASONING

	Use First	**Avoid**
What I think	What value does this have in the **real world?** I **figure out** how something works without using words. I don't want to read a book about it; I want to **get my hands on it.**	**Why should I care how this works?** Somebody has to **help me figure this out!** **Why do I have to make** something?
How I act	I charge in and **solve real problems.** I work in **my head and then with my hands.** I **tinker.**	**I avoid using tools or fixing**/repairing things. **I talk about it instead of doing** it. **I rely on reading the directions** in order to assemble a project.
What I feel	I feel **frustrated when the task has no real world relevance.** I enjoy competing with myself when **figuring out how something works.** I like the feel of **having the right tool** to get the job done.	I am **inept.** I feel **frustrated because I can't conceptualize the functions** involved in solving the issue. I am very **comfortable with my words and thoughts** - not tools.
My internal "chatter"	**Why am I required** to do this? I don't need to talk about it. I **already have it figured out.** I can't wait to **get my hands on this!**	**I don't care how it runs; I just want it to run!** I'm an educated person; I **should be able to solve this!** Why can't I **just talk or write about it?**

Table 3.3: TECHNICAL REASONING

Confluence

Confluence pulls together all areas of experience and forms them into new ideas and thoughts (Table 3.4). It is the Learning Process that allows you to see how concepts fit together. It is the Directional Force that enjoys taking a risk—enjoys going with your gut. This Learning Process has a sense, not a measurable sense, but an intuitive sense of how to proceed. Its internal message is frequently, "Don't be afraid to fail. You can always start again with a new idea."

Words that signal the need to use Confluence when completing a task or an assignment include: **Act carefree, brainstorm, concoct, create, dream-up, make-up, imagine, improve, innovate, invent, originate, risk, take a chance**.

Someone with Use First Confluence will generate many ideas and want to implement them all. This is a learner who embraces both the big picture and risk taking. Team members who are high in Confluence generate creative ideas and concepts, but often times those who Avoid Confluence or are Use as Needed aren't comfortable with what they perceive as "off the wall" thinking.

While these Learning Processes are universal across race, gender, and ethnicity, their make-up and use is very person-specific (Johnston & Dainton, 1996). Research indicates that most of us do not use all Learning Processes with equal comfort (Johnston, 1994). We may maximize our use of one or more of them and use others only as needed—and we may avoid one or more of them. Working as a team

CONFLUENCE

	Use First	Avoid
What I think	I think to **risk is to learn.** I think **outside the box.** I **connect things that are seemingly unrelated.**	Has this been well thought out? **I hate brainstorming!** **Where is this heading?**
How I act	I take risks and **push the boundaries.** I **brainstorm.** I read over, under, around and **between the lines.**	**I don't take risks without a plan.** **I avoid improvising** at the last minute. I can't follow "outside of the box" thinking.
What I feel	I am **not afraid to fail.** I **feel energized by possibilities** that are still in the idea stage. I revel in **connecting the dots!**	I feel **unsettled.** I feel **left out because I can't come up with ideas fast enough.** This is **out of control!** No **more changes or surprises,** please!
My internal "chatter"	**Nothing ventured, nothing gained.** I have **an idea. No, wait! I have an even better idea!** Think **Big Picture!**	Let's not lose sight of the plan. **Stay focused!** **Where did that idea come from?** Get a grip! Let's **deal with current realities** not fantasies!

Table 3.4: CONFLUENCE

of mental processes, they form a vibrant relationship that you can feel at work in you and that others can observe readily. Most important, your Directional Forces are your Directional Forces. There is no combination that is stronger; there is no combination that is weaker. Each Directional Force is of equal value, and all combinations are worthy of respect.

The point is that whatever the combination of Directional Forces, learners use all four Learning Processes simultaneously and to varying degrees. As noted throughout this chapter, the Directional Forces of your Compass Rose do not operate in isolation. They are purposely interactive (See Figure 3.5).

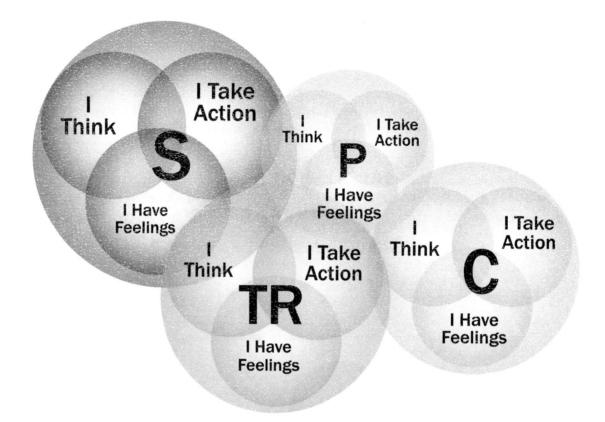

Figure 3.5: Twelve Interacting Spheres
The interaction of Learning Patterns within an individual
involves 12 separate mental processes converging on a single task.

Each Directional Force is of equal value, and all combinations are worthy of respect. The nature of the relationship among your Processes is the result of the number of you Use First, Use as Needed, and Avoid. Interestingly, not everyone has a Use First Pattern. Not everyone has an Avoid Pattern. Not everyone has a Use as Needed Pattern. Most have a combination of all three.

What follows is a description of different combinations. Read each carefully and compare the description to your combination of Learning Processes. Identify whether your combination of Directional Forces is Dynamic, Bridge, or Strong-Willed.

Dynamic Learner

If your Patterns form a Dynamic relationship, that means you **use at least one Pattern (but not more than two)** at the Use First level and the remainder of your Patterns consist of any combination of Use as Needed and Avoid Patterns. For example:

Sequence 17 (Avoid)
Precision 26 (Use First)
Technical Reasoning 30 (Use First)
Confluence 23 (Use as Needed)

Because of the different level of use among your Patterns, you can feel yourself shifting from the use of one Pattern to another. You sense when you are moving from a Use First to a Use as Needed Pattern. You feel the change based on your affective (emotive) response to the Pattern, and you recognize how your level of confidence is being affected, particularly when you move from your Use First Patterns to those you avoid. You can relate to others who share a similar connection among their Patterns, and you carry that awareness into your personal and work relationships.

Bridge Learner

If your Pattern combination consists of **no Use First** (scores of 25 to 35) **and no Avoid** (scores of 7 to 17), then you learn by using all of your Patterns at a Use as Needed level.

For example:
Sequence 21 (Use as Needed)
Precision 23 (Use as Needed)
Technical Reasoning 24 (Use as Needed)
Confluence 22 (Use as Needed)

Your Patterns form a bridge, creating the opportunity for the Patterns to work seamlessly to connect and solve learning challenges you face. *Three percent or less of the general population uses its Patterns in this manner.* When your patterns form a Bridge relationship, you are comfortable using all of them, but you feel no urgency to use one over another. Your Patterns serve a helpful role by leading from the middle.

One learner described his Bridge Patterns this way: "I don't need the spotlight; I just want to contribute in my quiet way. I learn by listening to others and interacting with them." Frequently, these individuals will say things such as, "I feel like a jack-of-all-trades and a master of none, but I find I can blend in, pitch in, and help make things happen as a contributing member of the group." "I weigh things in the balance carefully before I act." "I lead from the middle by encouraging others rather than taking charge of a situation."

These learners are team catalysts who, by listening and interacting with others, bring people closer to resolution while eliminating grandstanding and arguing. These individuals use phrases such as, "If I were you, I might consider. . .," and offer quiet alternatives rather than specific demands.

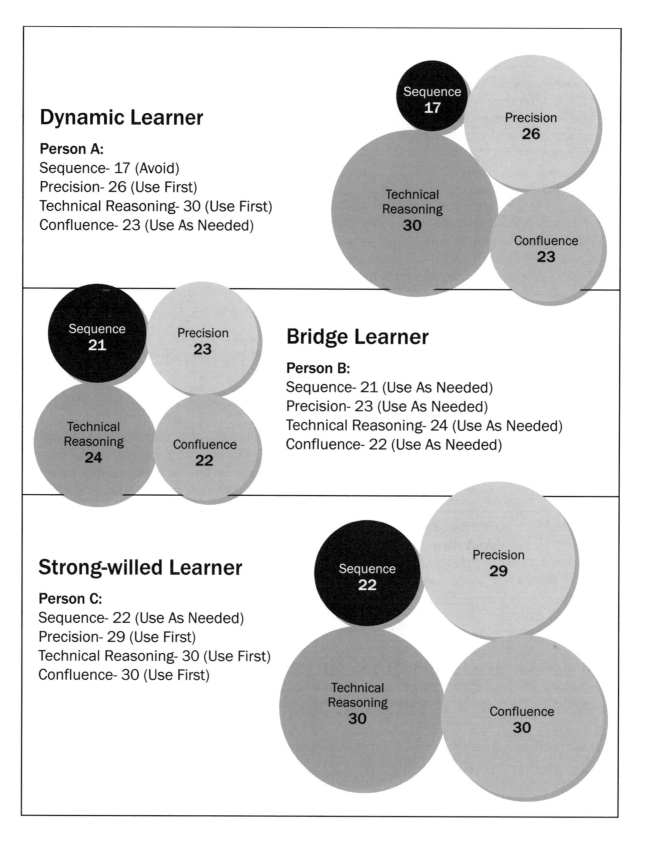

Dynamic Learner

Person A:
Sequence- 17 (Avoid)
Precision- 26 (Use First)
Technical Reasoning- 30 (Use First)
Confluence- 23 (Use As Needed)

Bridge Learner

Person B:
Sequence- 21 (Use As Needed)
Precision- 23 (Use As Needed)
Technical Reasoning- 24 (Use As Needed)
Confluence- 22 (Use As Needed)

Strong-willed Learner

Person C:
Sequence- 22 (Use As Needed)
Precision- 29 (Use First)
Technical Reasoning- 30 (Use First)
Confluence- 30 (Use First)

Figure 3.6: Pattern combinations vary in their degree of use of each of Learning Patterns.

Strong-Willed Learner

Much more common than the Bridge combination is **the learner who uses at least three or more Patterns at the Use First level and the remaining Pattern at the Use as Needed or Avoid level.** This combination of Patterns forms a Strong-Willed relationship among the Patterns. For example:

Sequence 22 (Use as Needed)
Precision 29 (Use First)
Technical Reasoning 30 (Use First)
Confluence 30 (Use First)

Approximately 25% to 30% of all persons fall under this description. These individuals seek out opportunities to lead rather than to be led. Their Directional Forces combination of three or more Use First Learning Processes positions them to be their own self-contained team. To confirm that your Learning Processes identify you as a Strong-Willed Learner, ask yourself the following questions:

- Do I experience a high degree of determination as a result of my multiple Use First Patterns?

- Do I prefer to control the plan, the ideas, the talks, the decisions, the processes, and the outcomes?

- Do I impose my way on others without recognizing what others have to offer?

If so, then be aware that your approach to leadership may cause peers, colleagues, family members, and teammates to question to what degree you value who they are and what they have to offer. Understanding yourself as a learner and being aware of how your approach is affecting those around you is particularly important when you have a Strong-Willed Pattern combination.

> **Your Learning Processes are who you are. They are right for you. They work well for you—when you know how to use them with intention.**

Because your Compass Rose can consist of any combination of the Use First, Avoid, and Use As Needed levels of Directional Forces, it is fascinating at times to observe how your Learning Processes operate in real life.

Directional Forces in Real Life: Stories of College Students

Early in this chapter I suggested that we each have our own story of learning shaped by our Directional Forces. Throughout this chapter you have had opportunities to read about and identify the four Learning Processes that comprise your Compass Rose. In the following pages, you will have the opportunity to read the stories of four individuals whose Learning Processes are quite evident. Use the four stories to hone your skills for recognizing the Directional Forces that make-up a person's Compass Rose and pay attention to how the different combinations of Learning Processes affect how willing learners are to take control and to use their Compass Rose with intention.

When You are Paralyzed by your Learning Processes

I can't get it all done.

Makayla is a quirky, funny, serious psychology student and an identical twin. Her Patterns of **Sequence 29, Precision 20, Technical Reasoning 17 and Confluence 14** do not match her twin's, by the way.

On the first day of the semester, Makayla was studiously attacking several information forms when the instructor moved on to a writing assignment. She assured students it was an ungraded sample, but that did nothing to lower Makayla's anxiety.

She said, "You want me to fill out the inventory. Then you want me to do this other form. Now you want me to write. Which is more important? I can't get it all done."

When time ran out and essays were collected, Makayla continued to write. She said, "Give me five more minutes."

The instructor said, "Don't worry. It's just a fast peek into who you are. Plus, there's another class coming in. We have to leave."

"I'll finish it in the hallway," she pleaded.

Makayla needed time to complete her work carefully, cautiously, and step-by-step. She steered away from any risks. She frequently emailed her instructor (often as she worked late into the night) for more instruction on assignments. She'd send paragraphs to her to be sure she was on the right track. Makayla was locked into her Sequence to the exclusion of her other Processes.

When you are Lt. Precision

Speaking of winning, I finally got my own room. It has spiders and the AC is weak and is right across from the port-a-potty so outside my door smells horrible, but it is a 6.5' x 6.5' space all my own.—John, Army scout

For families and friends with loved ones who are deployed, letters or emails are priceless. In John's email below, you will immediately recognize his high Precision (**Sequence 27, Precision 32, Technical Reasoning 21, Confluence 23**) found first in the glossary of acronyms he includes and then in the details he includes as he relates his daily life.

I'm at FOB Shank for a bit, transporting a guy's gear so that they can forward it to him back in Germany. Shank's pretty nice compared to BBK. They have running water, a bus service, and a sweet DFAC. I woke up to a spider crawling across my leg at 0200. It was not pleasant. It is, however, better than squatting in my office, which I have been doing for the last week and a half. Thanks to all the gear we wear, sunburn has not been an issue, but I'm pretty sure I could use my multicam jacket as a stand-alone shelter now with all the dried sweat and oils worked into it.

While this young lieutenant feels almost compelled to give details, those low in Precision may have already "checked out" from reading this. You may have found yourself thinking, "Who cares? I don't need to know all this." Knowing your audience is crucial for those who are high in their use of Precision.

When You are a Person of Few Words

In my mind, I see everything as a machine. When I look at something, I see how it works but I struggle to explain to others without pictures or physically moving or pointing. Usually I've been the guy who tags along but contributes little to the conversation. —Paul, physical science

As you might suspect, many science majors are Use First Technical Reasoning. Paul, is a "grease monkey" and proud of it. By his own admission, he NEVER took any class notes. He contended that he kept everything "in his head." However, when his lack of intentional use of his Learning Patterns **(Sequence 20, Precision 16, Technical Reasoning 33, Confluence 24)** earned him a failing grade for improper headings, incorrect fonts, not enough support from research for his ideas and not even formatting his papers or numbering his pages, he finally made an appointment to discuss things with his writing instructor.

She advised him to recognize that his avoidance of information and what he considered to be "lengthy" paragraphs could be what was leading to his failing grades. He sheepishly admitted he hadn't bothered reading the research he'd found in the library's databases, but had skimmed through the abstracts.

When You Let Your Confluence Run Amuck

I can be easily annoyed, but I don't worry very much. That's what makes me different. I plan to succeed by chance. —Raheem, sociology

Unfortunately his defining decision to follow a devil-may-care attitude was only bolstered by his Use First Confluence and his high Technical Reasoning. Raheem was a "man of few words" who decided to live by chance. And he was well on a pathway to failure.

His refusal to face his Learning Processes and to learn to use them with intention, resulted in his inability to remain as a viable student. Raheem had taken one too many chances and bet on the wrong approach to college.

While Raheem's story is not one of success, you can still learn a great deal-beginning with the insight that students who do not take into account how their Learning Processes affect their critical writing skills are at greater risk of failure.

Critical thinking, critical reading, and critical writing require scheduled, set-aside, focused time to think, read, study and write. Trying to achieve a degree without thinking, reading, studying and writing with intention keeps you from reaching your full potential.

Your Compass Rose and the Voyage Ahead

In these first three chapters, you have identified your True North, framed the Directional Forces of your personal Compass Rose, explored the components that make up your brain-mind connection, and established the degree of influence your Compass Rose has on your learning.

In the next three chapters, under the heading of "Staying the Course," you will be guided in developing additional tools to help you navigate your life and your learning.

Boxing the Compass

- Configuring your personal Compass Rose is essential to understanding how to navigate your life because all of life's ventures rely on your ability to use your Learning Processes well.
- Configuring your Compass Rose allows you to understand your learning behaviors and others' response to them.
- Configuring your Compass Rose is a personal and powerful experience.

Taking Stock

1) Think about two assignments that you have been given recently, one that was difficult for you and one that was easy. Look at the scores of the Directional Forces that make up your Compass Rose (your Learning Patterns) and use them to analyze why you found one task difficult and the other one easy.

2) Examine the following Personal Learning Profiles (See Figures 3.6 and 3.7). Then develop a written profile of your Compass Rose using the following as a model: (Note that you will fill in your actual LCI Scale Scores.) (See Worksheet 3.1)

- Begin by entering each of the Directional Forces (Sequence, Precision, Technical Reasoning, and Confluence) into the form.
- Next write a brief description of how you use that Learning Process in your college context and your personal life. Put the Learning Process descriptions you read about in this chapter into your own words.

A Description of My Personal Compass Rose

EXAMPLE 1

	Avoid	Use As Needed	Use First
Sequence	09		
Precision		21	
Technical Reasoning		19	
Confluence			33

EXPLANATION

Sequence:

I am a person who avoids directions. They just don't make sense to me. The most I can handle is a three-step process. After that, I prefer to figure it out on my own.

Precision:

I use precision as needed. While I read a lot, I don't read non-fiction, factual books. I do research and dig into information when I'm interested in a topic. I don't seek information just to know facts. I am not a walking almanac of minutia.

Technical Reasoning:

I use my technical as needed similar to my precision. The part of technical that I relate to best is being able to work by myself. I am a loner not a joiner. I want just the right tool to get the job done, and I love gadgets, but I am not interested in how things work nor am I interested in fixing things.

Confluence:

I use my confluence as the leader of my personal learning team. I never met an idea I didn't like. If I do something once, the second time it becomes overworked and the third time boring. I like the excitement of pushing the envelope.

Figure 3.7: Example A: A Personal Learning Profile

A Description of My Personal Compass Rose

EXAMPLE 2: C. Kane

	Avoid	Use As Needed	Use First
Sequence			25
Precision			24
Technical Reasoning			25
Confluent			26

EXPLANATION

Sequence:

I love and live my life by lists! No matter the type: to-do, daily tasks, workouts, and goal-achieving, I use them. Having lists help me stay organized and makes me feel accomplished once I have completed them. In the end it keeps me motivated and on a mission to succeed no matter the task at hand. This organizational habit has led to other parts of my life becoming more structured as well including keeping up on maintenance, arranging items, desk cleanliness, and much more.

Precision:

Like I stated previously, I am very organized in my life and feel this has influenced all four categories for me. For example, being this organized has led me to be very attentive and obsessive with making things get done a certain way to prevent failure and errors from occurring. This attention to detail leads me to review everything before submission and even correct work once I have noticed it, even if it leads to additional work. I also feel that no matter the mistake and how small and insignificant it might be, it needs to be fixed! (All it takes is one mistake/missed step to lead to catastrophic events causing destruction)

Technical Reasoning:

I might not be the "jack of all trades" some people are when it comes to mechanics, but no matter what I try to give it a shot in fixing it if it is something I believe I am capable of learning. This leads me to observe others as they are working on mechanical fixes and building so that I might be able to learn and do the task in the future. I feel that it is important that you must try, even if you do not succeed. Though I might not be the best at it, I love to build and sculpt in my spare time. I believe it is a good way to unwind and keep a positive attitude.

Confluence:

I consider myself to be very creative and willing to work outside the box as needed in order to achieve the overall goal. In today's society there are tons of new technological advances that increase the number of ways to do something and it is vital that as an individual you try alternate methods and see which works best. This creative approach can help separate you from others and can lead to new and better solutions to a problem. I also believe working with others, who might be creative as well and have different learning methods and approaches, can help increase productivity by seeing what new possibilities and innovations can be accomplished. In the end I like to be creative and try new things, as long as it doesn't lead to any unnecessary risks or harm to others.

Figure 3.8: Example B: A Personal Learning Profile

A Description of My Personal Compass Rose

	Avoid	Use As Needed	Use First
Sequence			
Precision			
Technical Reasoning			
Confluence			

EXPLANATION

Sequence:

Precision:

Technical Reasoning:

Confluence:

Worksheet 3.1: Personal Learning Profile Worksheet

Finding Your Way:
Setting the Course

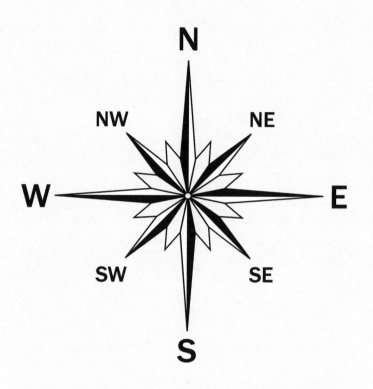

IV. ALL HANDS ON DECK

"The individual can fail, but the team cannot."
—Eugene Kranz (1977)
Mission Director, Apollo 13

The Focus

• Teaming our Directional Forces
• Understanding the internal talk of our learning

All hands on deck is a familiar nautical phrase that simply means the captain of the ship is facing a situation that calls for the entire crew's help. It declares the situation requires everyone's participation. For the learner, there's a term that means virtually the same thing. The term is **metacognition**, and like the cry *all hands on deck*, it too summons all of your mental processes—each Directional Force to be on alert and at the ready to take on the learning challenge that confronts you. Because of the centrality of metacognition to learning achievement, and because it remains an under-developed skill, this entire chapter focuses on it—what it means, how critical it is to your learning, and how best to develop its use with intention.

> **It is important for you to recognize that it is your ability to use your metacognition with intention that will determine whether you fail or succeed as a learner.**

The term metacognition literally means "an all encompassing gathering of thought." "Thinking about thinking," is its most common definition. However, in the context of the LML Advanced Learning System the definition of metacognition takes on a more robust and comprehensive meaning. Within LML, it is identified as a set of specific actions (the Metacognitive Drill) you can use that consciously assembles your Directional Forces *on deck* in real time and charges them to 1) talk with each other, 2) make strategic learning decisions in a cooperative manner, 3) and successfully solve the learning task that confronts you.

The following scenario represents an actual learning occurrence and reveals the nature of when and how an awareness of metacognition is called into play:

You have just been assigned a project that is going to require a strong use of Sequence, an equal amount of Precision, some Technical Reasoning, and virtually no Confluence. Your Directional Forces of Sequence 9, Precision 21, Technical Reasoning 19, and Confluence 33 do not match the task. As a result your Confluence (C 33) immediately begins to express its negative feelings about the fact that it is not being called upon to do the task. It feels limited and unappreciated. Trapped in a boring project. Your Use As Needed Precision and Technical Reasoning (P 21, TR 19) are disengaged wondering are they really needed? Up to the task? Meanwhile your Avoid Sequence (S09) has slunk away into the ship's hold of your mind filled with doubt and hoping not to be noticed. In other words, your Directional Forces have become directionless! Instead of all hands on deck you recognize you have no hands on deck.

Here is a classic example of how the intentional use of your metacognition can make all the difference in achieving your desired outcome. Because you understand metacognitively what is occurring and recognize these behaviors in yourself, you reissue your command for all hands on deck, and you take charge, talking back to your motley crew of Directional Forces and redirect them to complete the assignment successfully.

Here is the point: **only when you acknowledge and listen to your internal metacognitive chatter can you begin to take charge of your response to it.** The empowering, central point of *Finding Your Way* is that when you navigate your daily life aware of your Compass Rose and your metacognitive chatter—you can set a course and stay that course to a successful completion.

The empowering, central point of Finding Your Way *is that when you navigate your daily life aware of your Compass Rose and your metacognitive chatter—you can set a course and stay that course to a successful completion.*

The Story

This chapter's story focuses on an *all hands on deck* approach to solve the life or death challenge that faced the Apollo 13 space mission. The approach of Houston's communication, decision-making, problem-solving team's actions when confronted with an impending disaster mirrors the operations we need to employ as learners when confronted with an impending learning disaster. Read further and examine the parallels.

Most of us know the story of Apollo 13. Some of us lived every moment of it as we tracked the unfolding of what appeared to be a space voyage disaster in the making. Others know the story from its retelling in the movie *Apollo 13*. Those who saw the film remember one of its most dramatic moments. Facing the nearly impossible task of bringing the astronauts home despite the spacecraft's loss of oxygen and power, the support teams at the Houston Space Center were challenged to create equipment that would allow the astronauts to power up the craft using only the materials and equipment available to them. In the film, teams sorted through piles of disparate items dumped on a table in front of them, seeking to convert trash into functioning systems.

Although offering a less cinematic depiction of the situation, Michael Useem (1998), in his book, *The Leadership Moment*, relates the urgency of the situation as he describes how Eugene Kranz, the 36-year-old mission director, **communicated** and interacted with his various mission control teams. Constantly aware that this was a life-and-death situation, Kranz **drew on the knowledge and expertise of his team members, listened intently** to their minute-by-minute updates, **calculated the options**, and **weighed in the balance how to** avoid failure and **achieve a lifesaving outcome**.

Useem quotes Kranz as describing his job as "basically to orchestrate all the players" (p. 87) and to bring "the team together" (p. 80). Key insights can be gained from deconstructing the Apollo 13 story. These insights focus not only on the leadership of Kranz during the crisis, but even more on the preparation of teams led by Kranz prior to the launch and the ensuing crisis.

Much of Kranz's approach to teams is applicable to our internal metacognitive team of Learning Processes. In The Learning that follows, note the importance of listening to the various Processes in order to be able to use them **with intention** to solve any problem or dilemma that confronts you. This is the first step in using metacognition with intention and making it work for you. *All hands on deck!*

The Learning

What we learn from Apollo 13 is that to succeed when under duress, we need to have formed our Team Metacognition well. We need to know the Directional Forces that make up the team—including their assets, their expertise, how well they work with others, and we need to know their abilities and willingness to communicate. Then we need to do the following:

- Listen to them.
- Consult with them.
- Rehearse them thoroughly under a variety of circumstances.
- Make them interchangeable.
- Use their insights strategically to inform our decisions.

The Apollo 13 story lends itself well to understanding how to use our internal team of Learning Processes to navigate our lives. Just as mission control did, you and I need to know what the makeup of our team of Learning Processes is, understand how the pieces communicate with one another, and recognize the expertise each brings to a given situation. When we listen to the internal talk of our Learning Processes, our metacognitive team, we are able to harness the pull of our True North to the directional guidance of our Compass Rose, and set ourselves on a course that will succeed.

I cannot overemphasize this point. Taking time to listen to your team of Learning Processes is vital. Listening is more than hearing. It is the conscious processing of what you hear. True listening yields attentiveness and allows you to weigh in the balance the perspectives you are hearing so you can then act. Think back to the story of Raheem, our devil-may-care, "I don't need a stinking plan," student from Chapter III. How well did he listen to his Directional Forces? His instructor? More significantly, consider, how well did he succeed?

Missing the Message of Team Metacognition

Often we miss the voice of our metacognition because we are over stimulated with ringtones, blasting video games, text notifications, or deafening music. We spend a great deal of time trying not to hear—not to listen to our minds at work. To ignore that conversation is to say to the Compass Rose of our learning, "I am not interested in your directional voice. I am going to drown you out with excuses and busyness. Give me a single straightforward message, not a series of whispers and shouts all tangled together."

To an extent, we do have a right to ask our metacognition to clarify its message. It would be so simple if we heard one, clear, direct instruction. But we don't because our mind, our Compass Rose of Directional Forces, does not speak with one liners. Our metacognition doesn't speak with one voice, but is comprised of a quartet of tones. It challenges us to hear the harmony and disharmony; it alerts us to potential discord within us or among the people with whom we are working. It forces us to listen and to then make defining decisions.

If my Sequence is crying out that it is over-whelmed (too many balls in the air or not a clear enough outline of a project or assignment, for example), I need to hear that. If my Confluence is seeking attention by pumping one idea on top of another at the risk of keeping me from moving forward or from meeting a deadline, I need to acknowledge it while taking action to turn down its volume (focus and go forward). I need to salve my hurting Sequence and find a means to strengthen it for the task ahead.

Hearing metacognition within us takes practice, patience, and skill. By using your crew of Learning Processes, you will be using the most powerful personal navigational tool you possess. You will have at your ready your thinking skills, your power to act, and your True North embedded in each aspect of your decisions. There is no more powerful combination of human resources for directing your life journey.

Listening to Your Metacognition and Attending to Its Midcourse Corrections

Metacognition consists of the voices of your Learning Processes as they seek to resolve how to plot a course for success. Metacognition, however, is not passive. It is active, constantly checking to see if you are on or off course. It does so through a series of phases, a continuum of activities that help you check your progress and position you to stay the course. I have ascribed action verbs to represent each phase of metacognition: (See Figure 4.2.)

- Mull   asks you to consider, "What am I supposed to be doing?"
- Connect   asks you to recall, "Have I ever done this or something similar?"
- Rehearse   asks you to practice, "Let me see if I can do this."
- Attend   asks you to stay focused, "Let me concentrate and not be distracted."
- Express   asks you to perform the task, "Go public. Turn in the assignment!"
- Assess   asks you to evaluate yourself, "How did I do? Did I put forth effort?"
- Reflect   asks you to face yourself, "What did I do? What did I fail to do?"
- Revisit   asks you to reconsider, "How could I improve the outcome next time?"

Most often, we plot our course by using our metacognitive action phases in a specific order. However, because the degrees to which we use our Directional Forces differ, the manner in which we use our metacognition also differs. We sometimes begin at the beginning and Mull, but other times we jump into a situation in the middle and just begin to Express. As you read through the explanation of each term, you will be able to identify specific instances when you have used all or some of the phases in or out of order.

Mull

Virtually all tasks begin with some form of **Mulling**. "What am I being asked to do? Have I ever done this before? What were the results? Do I want to repeat those results or avoid them?" *You stay firmly anchored until you have a sense of where you are going and how you are going to prepare for the venture.* Mulling is healthy; stewing isn't. Don't let your mind become so frustrated because you don't understand the assignment that you allow yourself to give up. If the voices of your Directional Forces are crying out for clearer directions or a greater sense of purpose, then listen to them and ask for what you need.

Connect

If you have Mulled successfully, then almost seamlessly you begin to make Connections to the requirements of the task. You collect your thoughts, review your options, and prepare for the venture. You gather your resources, talk with others who may have taken on a similar task, compare your task to theirs, note the differences and similarities, and begin to accumulate the resources you will need to support and sustain your plan. The **Connect** aspect of your metacognition has your Pattern of Sequence working diligently and your Pattern of Precision equally hustling, scouring for pertinent data. Your Technical Reasoning is in survival mode while your Confluence is holding back because it doesn't enjoy basing the future on the past. It would much rather skip the Connecting phase and get to the make-or-break action. If you are wise, you will ignore the folly offered by your Confluence and allow your other Patterns to guide you in connecting fully and completely with the task at hand.

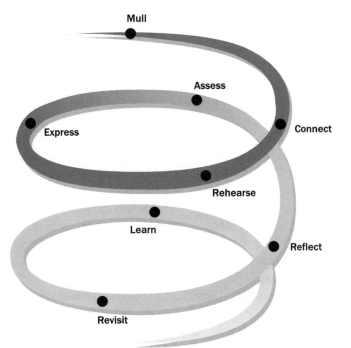

Mull	asks you to consider, "What am I supposed to be doing?"
Connect	asks you to recall, "Have I ever done this or something similar?"
Rehearse	asks you to practice, "Let me see if I can do this."
Attend	asks you to stay focused, "Let me concentrate and not be distracted."
Express	asks you to perform the task, "Go public. Turn in the assignment!"
Assess	asks you to evaluate yourself, "How did I do? Did I put forth the effort."
Reflect	asks you to face yourself, "What did I do? What did I fail to do?"
Revisit	asks you to reconsider, "How could I improve the outcome next time?"

Figure 4.2: By working through the phases of the Metacognitive Drill, the learner becomes more intentional and more engaged in the learning process.

Rehearse-Attend

The next metacognitive checkpoint for course corrections involves two joint phases, **Rehearse-Attend**. The Rehearse phase allows your Patterns to go through a trial run in your head to make certain that the performance of the task, the completion of the project, and/or the public presentation of the outcomes will meet the standards originally set. Rehearsal prepares for expression by allowing any mistakes to be assessed and corrected. This is where your Sequence will shine to whatever degree it comprises your Compass Rose and your Precision will work to take corrective action.

The **Attend** phase of metacognition is when you need to be coaching, encouraging, and challenging your Learning Processes to be on alert and to continue doing the work of intentional learning. Attending to a learning task is to be in an active state of focus, clearing away distractions, and concentrating on what you need to consciously do to complete the task well. To Attend means you don't let up; you'll continue to operate at a high level of focused energy. The reason this is so important is that when you submit your work or complete an assessment, or in any way perform the action that you have been rehearsing, you want it to occur at the same high level of performance that you achieved during the rehearsal phase.

Express

Expression, actually doing what was practiced, is the "going public" part of the cycle. Expression is no longer the test run but the real thing. Although your Processes of Sequence and Precision particularly enjoyed Rehearsal, they are not at ease during the **Express** phase.

You will hear a greater tension in the internal talk of Sequence and Precision. They want their Rehearsal to pay off with perfection. **Rehearse-Attend-Express** is their mantra. Technical Reasoning, on the other hand, is fired up because the long awaited time for action has finally arrived! Meanwhile, Confluence, which was yawning during Rehearsal and questioning how many times you have to go over the same thing, is ready to Express! In fact, Use First Confluence would much prefer to do this live, with no Rehearsal, no safety nets, and no lifeboats.

During this metacognitive phase, Confluence is not bounded by the compunction of Precision for perfection. If you are aware of how the voice of Confluence can, like the Sirens of Greek mythology, seek to pull you off course, then you will be able to quiet their influence and hold steady to the course of Rehearse-Express. In fact, you will prepare fully and completely for any and all exigencies.

The final phases of metacognition join with the initial phases to create a reflective practice feedback loop. When you enter into these phases, you are in both a vulnerable and an enviable position. If you sail through this set of phases unscathed, then you have, indeed, used your Compass Rose well, allowing you not only to stay your course but also to come safe home. On the other hand, missteps and challenges along the way will help you learn how to empower your course correction capacity for the next learning voyage.

Assess

Metacognition, when faithfully followed, will always include a time to **Assess**. Unlike external assessment or "testing," the Assess of metacognition means confronting questions such as, "What have I really achieved?" and "To what degree have I achieved it?" Jim Collins (2001), in *Good to Great*, refers to this as facing your current reality. What is the outcome of your effort? What are the quantitative and qualitative results? This is when you need to let the data lead you to confront what was achieved as a result of your efforts. The metacognitive phase that follows focuses on the words of the prior question, "as a result of your efforts," because reflection requires a long hard look at yourself.

Reflect

When you **Reflect** you ask, "Where does the buck stop? Who is responsible for this success? This failure? This mess?" This is the piece of professional and personal growth you may have been missing. You see, anyone can use the phrase, "mistakes have been made," to attribute failure and blame anonymously. But only mindful individuals with a clear sense of their personal True North and Compass Rose of Directional Forces can face their self-imposed mirror and say precisely, "I screwed up, and I am prepared to take the heat for it." Interestingly, this is where Technical Reasoning can assume too much responsibility, believing that it is the sole factor that determines the success or failure of an operation. It is important to examine the contribution of each Directional Force to one's success or failure—to consider the totality of the effect of Team Metacognition on the final outcome (Johnston, 2006; Jha, A. P., Stanley, E.A., & Baime, M. J. 2010).

Using your metacognition well equips you to stay the course of your metacognitive phases until you reach a powerful self-awareness. It is only if you stay the course and reflect that you become willing to ask, "Confronted with the same situation, what would I personally do differently? How would I recalculate, rethink, re-plot, and reequip?" With a new maturity and sense of self, you can do this without ever pointing to anyone but yourself and reflecting on the outcome.

You are now ready to use reflective practice to ask which of the espoused values of your True North you abandoned along the way. Ask yourself the following: What did I allow myself to do? What did I allow myself to fail to do? Where did my Compass Rose, my Directional Learning Processes, steer me off course?

This is the autopsy of failure. Without it you are doomed to continue to achieve less than you could. You cannot continue to repeat your actions, believing that they will yield a different outcome. Interestingly, this is where our Confluence can lead us because Confluence understands failure. Confluence learns from failure in a manner that it does not from the Connecting and Rehearsal phases since it frequently chooses to ignore or skip them completely. Confluence, when confronted with failure, immediately and willingly seeks to understand what, in retrospect, it could not grasp in the planning phase. Listen to the Confluence of your Compass Rose, and let it lead you fearlessly through this vital phase.

Reflection requires us to face ourselves, specifically the totality of who we are and how we have used our Compass Rose, our metacognitive talk, and our self-correcting opportunities or how we have failed to do so. This is the heart of *Finding Your Way*.

Revisit

The good news found in reflective practice is that it does not conclude with assigning blame and shame or with rewarding success. Instead, reflective practice invites you to **Revisit** your metacognitive phases, noting both those that enriched and those that frustrated your venture. Revisiting metacognitive decisions serves to reinforce the specific strategies that led to success and reconsider those that led to failure. Revisiting grows metacognitive capacity and personal insight (Osterman & Kottkamp, 2004).

You may have noted that at each stage of the metacognitive spiral (Mull, Connect, Rehearse-Attend, Express, Assess, Reflect, and Revisit)—the conversation among your Directional Forces changes—actually develops and evolves. The more frequently we tune in to them, the more clearly we can identify the guidance they are providing us as a team.

Putting the Learning into Practice

The proactive use of your **Metacognition** is essential if you are operating in a college learning environment. For example, a typical college assignment involves writing of some type. Your Team Metacognition helps you understand that a writing task isn't just a "simple putting down of your thoughts on paper." Instead, the task requires a sophisticated use of your brain-mind connection and your metacognitive team. Whether handwritten or word processed, writing requires you to put your thoughts into symbolic representation (letters). The symbols you choose need to form words that have the same meaning each time they are viewed by the human eye and translated by the brain's neuro-receptors. Their meaning and intent must stay consistent even after they have passed through your Learning Processes to those of another person. They must represent the same tone, message, and perspective that you intended.

Viewed from this perspective, writing suddenly becomes a set of brain-mind challenges. So although the task might be to write a brief summary of a lecture or an assigned reading or a lab experiment, the task is not a simple one! It is the metacognition of our Compass Rose that navigates the issues confronting us when we are working to complete a task such as this. Take, for instance, the assignment to write a 200 word summary of an assigned reading. And let's say that your Compass Rose is one that Avoids Precision and uses Technical Reasoning at the Use First level (Sequence 22, Precision 15, Technical Reasoning 28, and Confluence 23).

A writing task is typically the last thing you will want to complete. The procrastination is simply one way of putting off your struggle with words. Those who Avoid Precision don't like dealing with words, and will find it difficult to discern the most important facts or information to convey because they all seem equally important and equally overwhelming; those who are Use First Technical Reasoning relish working in other symbol forms and declare that words aren't their tool of choice. Combined, these two Processes can make the task seem monumental. Here is where your awareness of your metacognitive team can be helpful.

Your Compass Rose as a Team Effort

First, instead of waiting to be rescued, you can pull yourself out of the doldrums and make your way by looking to the other Directional Forces that make up your Compass Rose. Yes, it's true that you have two that seem to be working against you (Precision 15 and Technical Reasoning 28) when it comes to completing the task, but you also have two other Patterns that will help you listen (Sequence 22 and Confluence 23). So far, their voices have been muffled by the whining of your Avoid Precision and Use First Technical Reasoning. However, to ignore these other members of your team is to flounder when you could be sailing through the task.

Here is how your other two Processes can contribute. Because your Confluence is at the high side of Use As Needed, let's look at it first as a possible place to start. Interestingly, your Confluence offers an idea for where to begin. It suggests to your team of Directional Forces that you can employ your Use As Needed Sequence to organize three specific points to record as the most significant pieces of information to come out of the meeting. Your Sequence also suggests that you Revisit the agenda for the meeting to identify the key points you need to recount, thereby rescuing your Avoid Precision from having to determine what to include in the report and what to leave out. Because of this efficient way of approaching the task, your Technical Reasoning suddenly seems energized. It can see the purpose in what you are doing. Meanwhile, your Precision begins to come alive, feeling less and less overwhelmed.

This is teamwork in action! Is this is a lot to consider? Yes. Important to consider? Vital! Possible to understand? Absolutely! Can it make all the difference in whether you stay the course and complete the task successfully? Yes, indeed. In fact using your metacognition as a team and with intention is critical for success in all learning situations (Lovett, 2008).

What does that mean? It means that you build your plan for completion of a learning task using your awareness of yourself as a learner and an awareness of what you are being called upon to do. Your plan includes not just a timeline or a list of the steps you need to complete. It also includes a set of strategies to shape your learning actions so that they fit you as a learner and match up well with the requirements of the assignment (See Table 4.1.). Chapter V will expand upon the application of these techniques and help you build your skills aimed at reducing your non-productive learning behaviors and replacing them with metacognitively-based learning behaviors.

Nonproductive learning behaviors	Metacognitive-based learning behaviors
You read words without filtering or studying the content for accuracy.	You use your Precision to read the assigned pages and analyze the information for accuracy.
You have information and repeat it without considering its source.	You use your Precision to formulate your opinion and then turn to your Sequence to organize your thoughts to determine if the information is balanced and well referenced.
You read and memorize information without considering its value or importance.	You use your Technical Reasoning to gain an understanding of what you have read and to apply that understanding to different situations in your life. For example, you ask how relevant and practical it is. You determine how you can use it as a student as well as a young professional.
You skim the readings and look at the graphics without reading for depth.	You use your Team Metacognition to examine the text (Precision); you connect the graphics and figures to what you are reading (Technical Reasoning); you formulate your own thoughts about what you have read (Confluence).
You complete the assignment and move on to the next task without understanding its purpose or link to future learning.	You use your Sequence to follow the Metacognitive Drill going back and reviewing your learning the experience, noting what you have learned and what you would do differently the next time you have a similar assignment (Revisit).
You turn the assignment in and wait for feedback without doing any personal evaluation of its quality.	Before turning in the assignment, you use Team Metacognition to revisit how you completed it and whether you used your Learning Processes appropriately so that the assignment has caused you to grow in knowledge, skill, and judgment.

Table 4.1.: Nonproductive v. Metacognitively-Based Learning Behaviors

The metacognitive based behaviors described in Table 4.1 reinforce the importance of knowing the use for each aspect of your Directional Forces both as individual processes and as a team. As you reviewed the list of behaviors, did any, either non-productive or productive, seem to be describing you?

Throughout this chapter you have been learning the importance of finding your way through the use of your metacognition. By now it has become very clear that an all hands on deck use of your metacognition takes work. The work is worthwhile, however, because it equips you to do the work of learning and to do it well. Moreover, when you understand your metacognition, you are well equipped, "to consistently enhance your capacity to produce results that are truly important to you" (Senge, 1999, p. 45).

Boxing the Compass

- What metacognition teaches us is that each of our Directional Forces (Learning Processes) has a voice that is available to us and that can help us navigate any task, assignment, or project.
- Meanwhile, our metacognition guides our course and plots any midcourse corrections should the need arise.

Taking Stock

1) Think about the last time you had a really bad feeling when you were given an assignment. Using your new understanding of your Learning Processes and the internal talk that each uses, can you identify what conflict among your Processes might have been causing you to have that reaction?

2) Think about a time when you were experiencing a lot of metacognitive internal talk. Was it positive and empowering or was it negative? Develop a graphic representation that would explain the internal talk, noting the various metacognitive phases you were in as you worked your way through the situation. Label aspects of the visual with the metacognitive terms that follow: Mull, Connect, Rehearse, Attend, Express, Assess, Reflect, Revisit, and Learn.

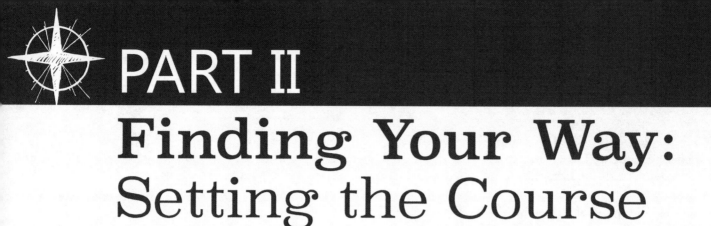

PART II
Finding Your Way:
Setting the Course

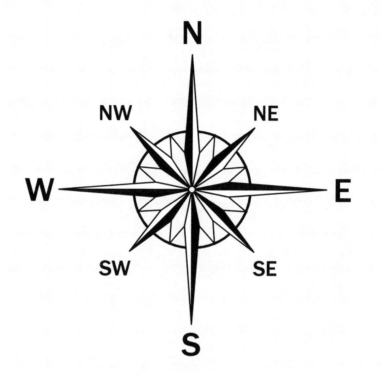

V. ADRIFT IN UNCHARTED WATERS

"We need a better understanding of how we learn so we can breakthrough and handle the learning punches that come at us everyday."
—Dr. Stephen Lehmkuhle, Chancellor,
University of Minnesota Rochester

The Focus

- *Understanding the power contained in one's Compass Rose*
- *Understanding the strategic use of one's personal learning tools*

Being required to operate in **uncharted waters** confronts us daily. When you find yourself in uncharted waters, you are in a situation that is unfamiliar to you. As you have no experience with it, you don't know what outcome to expect. In other words, "Destination unknown. Navigation unclear. Outcome in doubt." It's more than an unplanned disruption in a well-planned day. It's more than facing the unexpected. It involves *being required to perform well doing something that is unfamiliar.* Uncharted waters are what most frequently appear to make our lives, our work, and our relationships operate under stress. Uncharted waters are the unexpected, unanticipated, and the "no directions attached" aspects of our lives.

It might be something as simple as taking a required course in a subject area where you have no knowledge and even less interest. It might entail being assigned a major project requiring you to work with people you have never teamed with before. Or it might be something as major as moving cross country to obtain employment. Just the thought of making such a move acts as "a real learning punch" that can throw you off course. And make no mistake, when uncharted waters confront you, the key predictor of whether you fail or succeed—is how you take in the situation and make sense of it *vis* a *vis* who you are as a learner. Here is an example of what uncharted waters look like in a learning situation:

> *A student medical lab tech is being tested on her clinical procedures. With her high Sequence, high Precision, and avoidance of Confluence, she is having difficulty solving problems similar, but not identical, to ones she has practiced and successfully completed during earlier labs. She sits without speaking, trying to recall, "Where have I seen this exact question before? What did I do to respond to it correctly?" After five minutes of total brain freeze, she worriedly whispers to a fellow student, "I don't know what to do here."*

The problem facing her requires that she connect her prior experience to a similar problem— the one in front of her. The emphasis here is on the word similar, as opposed to exact. The student is paralyzed because she can't remember an exact problem to duplicate. She has the intelligence and the skills required to solve the problem, but she can't call up the confidence to direct them to the question at hand because she is stuck in the Connecting phase of her metacognition. Her Directional Forces (Use First Precision and Sequence) keep her fixated on the need to solve an *identical* problem when in fact she need only recall a *similar* problem. When individuals with this Compass Rose of Directional Forces don't see that they can carry insights from one type of problem to another, they flounder in what they **perceive** as *uncharted waters.*

In the previous four chapters, you have been preparing to face the challenge of uncharted waters. In Chapter Four you learned the importance of your metacognitive team and how to put it to use to complete a task, to make midcourse corrections, and to persist until you reach your destination. This chapter focuses on using your Directional Forces to "take the punches" that confront you whether as a college student or someone entering into a new career. In this chapter you have an opportunity to take your self-awareness and discover how to position yourself logistically and strategically to take on the uncharted aspects of your college learning (Ornstein & Thompson, 1984).

The story that follows demonstrates how one college student, having taken a significant "learning punch" that caused him to doubt his abilities to succeed in his college writing course, employed the power of his Directional Forces (Compass Rose) and the specific personal learning tools of decoding and strategizing to navigate uncharted waters.

The Story

Steven

Sequence: 27   **Precision: 19**   **Technical Reasoning: 33**   **Confluence: 23**

Both of the writing pieces that I have written for this year in College Comp have come back with a big C+ on them. This is not a grade I am used to viewing in any class, yet I am not totally surprised. I am not prepared for this writing class.

The way my brain functions does not allow me to easily compose an amazing essay. Also, I have never had a teacher that attempted to correct my writing style or graded tough enough to force me to put more work behind my writing. I don't have this problem with the writing pieces for Advanced College Chemistry, or Engineering Clinic. All writing pieces for chemistry and clinic are very sequential. Every single piece follows the same exact format, and this is what my professors in those classes like. I find these pieces easy to compose. Therefore, I've concluded that my problem with writing essays for College Comp must rest in that there are no set boundaries and directions to follow. In fact, I usually lose the most points for writing the essay in a far too sequential way.

In order to begin fixing this essay writing dilemma, I should begin to use the proper steps to writing an essay that I have usually skipped without consequence. The first would be to write the body and then go back and write the introduction and conclusion. This is a very hard thing to do for someone with such high Sequence, but it will lead to a better overall introduction and conclusion.

The second step I must take is to think deeper about the problem at hand. Usually I get started on a paper and write until I hit the page requirement. My Confluence must be intensified to allow for better out-of-the-box ideas.

The third step and probably the most important is to proofread more. Every essay so far this year has come back with awkward sentence structure, missing transitions, and grammar errors. For someone with use as needed Precision, it is hard for me to even read my own writing. I become bored very quickly.

Knowing these things about myself, I have begun to apply the following changes: *My first course of action was on a rewrite for one of my papers that I received a C+ on. This time around, I proofread the entire paper myself to fix all errors in grammar, sentence structure, awkward sentences, and tense that I could find. I then thought deeper about the paper. Since it was about an advertisement I had created, I asked myself some questions: What is the first thing the viewer will notice? Is it too busy? Who is this ad trying to attract? These questions allowed me to think deeper about my advertisement and create some stronger arguments.*

These new insights and methods for writing my essays have also taught me many things about my Learning Processes and how they have to be adjusted specifically to meet the requirements of my College Comp course. *My Learning Processes have to adjust when I sit down to write an essay. My Sequence has to be tethered to a Use as Needed ability, and my Technical Reasoning needs to not only be tethered but ball and chained. I feel the pain of having to do this every time I try and write.*

I cannot feel like proofreading is a waste of time anymore, and I must begin writing as someone with higher Precision. It is part of my life. It must get done. The biggest step I can take from now on is to hand my paper out to a friend for a peer review. This will give me a second perspective on my writing. I will be best off to find someone with high Precision to do this review of my writing. **My learning ability is my own, and it must be used thoughtfully so that I can continue to do well in whatever field I attempt.**

The Learning

Steve did an amazing job of responding to the "learning punches" he faced in his Comp. I class. By using the tools of Decoding and Fitting, Steve overcame what had been for him an unsuccessful learning experience. You too can develop your own personal learning tools and use them effectively to navigate the uncharted waters presented by an unfamiliar problem, daunting task, or frustrating situation.

You too can develop your own personal learning tools and use them effectively to navigate uncharted waters.

The Tool of Decoding

The first and most practical tool you can develop is called Decoding. It is used to analyze an assignment or task in terms of what skills and Learning Processes will be required to successfully complete the task. The goal of Decoding an assignment is twofold: (1) to identify and clarify the intent of the directions (i.e., what exactly are the direction-giver's expectations for the outcome of the assignment); and (2) to identify how you are going to need to fit your Learning Processes to the task in order to complete the assignment as per the directions.

The first step to navigating *uncharted waters* is to Decode the task accurately. The more involved the requirements, the more important it is that you decode the assignment before starting. At this point, you may be thinking that this is a great deal of work just to understand what appears to be a straightforward task. And that may be true if you've successfully completed a similar task before and your Learning Processes match the requirements of the current task.

But let's consider what could occur if your Directional Forces, your Learning Processes, are a mismatch to the task? What if you have concerns that your instructor and you seem to be coming from different learning planets and your Directional Forces clearly do not match? How will you meet your instructor's expectations? What if the assignment calls for a heavy use of Sequence (*organize* and chart each participant's *daily schedule*) and you happen to Avoid Sequence? Will the way you use your Sequence be sufficient to accomplish the task to your clinical instructor's standards?

The tool of Decoding requires us to understand our personal Directional Forces and use them to take specific action to complete a task. Using Decoding, we can deconstruct assignments, objectives, or any set of directions. Using the example that follows, examine the steps for Decoding an assignment. (See Figure 5.2):

Step 1. Read the following assignment carefully:

Using the data below, construct a graph that shows the percentage of car accidents for drivers from ages 17 to 25.

Step 2. Re-read it a second time, this time underlining key words such as the verbs, proper nouns, specific numbers or amounts, adjectives or adverbs that further describe what specifically you are expected do.

<u>Using</u> the <u>data</u> provided, <u>construct a graph</u> that shows the <u>percentage</u> of car <u>accidents</u> for <u>drivers</u> from <u>ages 17 to 25</u>.

Step 3. Make a list of the words you circled.

- Using (Use)
- Data
- Construct
- Graph
- Percentage
- Drivers
- 17-25

Step 4. Now locate each word you underlined on the Learning Process Word Wall (See Figure 5.3). Note under which of Learning Process sectors the word is found.

Step 5. Next to each word on your list, designate what Learning Process it falls under. For example, the very first word you listed was *Using*, a derivative of the word Use. Use is found on the Word Wall under the Technical Reasoning quadrant. Continue identifying the Directional Force of each until all are labeled. You have now completed the *decoding* of your task.

Without your awareness of your Compass Rose and without experience in the use of Decoding, you may find yourself shutting down or submitting a lab notebook that earns you less than a stellar grade. However, if you have learned to Decode tasks first, you are able to make strategic moves to keep your Directional Forces focused on how to complete the task successfully.

Or suppose you are required to keep a lab log and turn it in to be graded as a test. Your Precision is 21. It does what it needs to do. Like the Goldilocks syndrome, it's not too little or too much. It's just right. But you begin to recognize after the second week of class that your instructor's Precision is at least a Use First and probably in the Upper Range of 30 plus. You have no prior experience in keeping a lab log, and you have never had a class with an instructor as high in Precision as yours is. You find yourself lost in *uncharted water*. You begin to think, "Will the amount of information I logged be enough? Will it match the instructor's expectation for "A" level work?"

Using (Use) TR
Data P
Construct TR

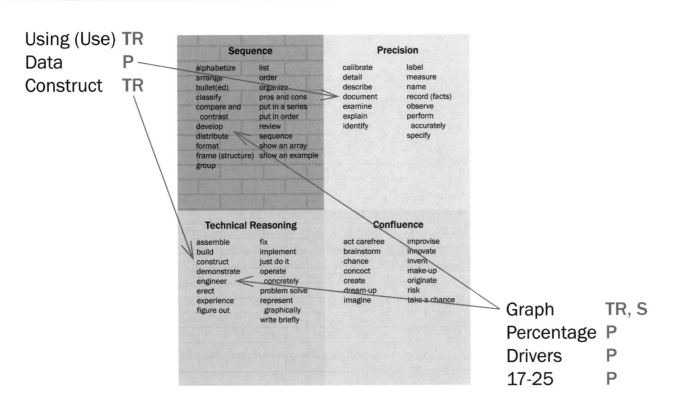

Graph TR, S
Percentage P
Drivers P
17-25 P

Figure 5.2: Decoding an Assignment: The more involved the requirements, the more important it is that you decode the assignment before starting.

Learning Process Word Wall: Use these words to help you decipher assignments, questions, and projects.

Sequence

- alphabetize
- arrange
- bullet(ed)
- classify
- compare and contrast
- contextualize
- demonstrate
- develop
- distribute
- double check
- focus on a theme
- follow directions
- follow a logical progression
- format
- frame (structure)
- group
- list
- order
- organize
- practice
- pros and cons
- put in chronological order
- put in a series
- put in order
- review
- revisit
- sequence
- show an array
- show an example
- structure
- summarize
- tell a story (beginning, middle, and end)
- transition

Precision

- argue
- assess
- be accurate
- be exact
- calibrate
- cite
- detail
- determine
- describe
- document
- evaluate
- examine
- explain
- identify
- label
- measure
- name
- narrate using details
- number
- read
- record (facts)
- observe
- perform accurately
- persuade
- refine
- specify
- use facts
- write

Technical Reasoning

- assemble
- build
- construct
- demonstrate
- engineer
- erect
- experience
- figure out
- find a reasonable answer
- fix
- implement
- just do it
- operate concretely
- problem solve
- represent graphically
- use words sparingly
- use logic
- write concisely

Confluence

- act carefree
- brainstorm
- chance
- concoct
- create
- dream-up
- ideate (come up with ideas)
- imagine
- improvise
- improvise
- infer
- innovate
- invent
- make-up
- originate
- predict
- pretend
- risk
- take a chance

Figure 5.3: Learning Process Word Wall: Use these words to help you decode assignments, questions, and projects.

Now it's your turn to move into uncharted waters and decode a task. As you read and complete the decoding task, observe how the Word Wall guides you to accurately label the key words contained in the task's directions.

Literature Assignment

Write a brief, bulleted summary of the assigned reading from Maya Angelou's, *Wouldn't Take Nothing for My Journey Now*. Your summary should include key points but should not exceed 250 words. I am seeking your first impression, not an encyclopedic analysis of the text.

First, Decode and label the key words of the task. Next, analyze the degree to which you will be required to use your Learning Processes to complete each aspect of the work assignment. Then ask what type and amount of Directional Forces are going to be required to complete the task? Can you identify the point when you will need to be using one portion of your Compass Rose more than another?

To see the correctly decoded task, look below and examine how the key terms of the task were identified and labeled.

<u>Write</u> a <u>brief, bulleted summary</u> of the assigned reading from <u>Maya Angelou's, Wouldn't Take Nothing for My Journey Now</u>. Your summary should <u>include key points</u> but should <u>not exceed 250 words</u>. I am seeking your <u>first impression, not an encyclopedic analysis</u> of the text.

List of key words:
Sequential Words
- Bulleted
- Points
- Summary

Precise Words
- Write
- Title of reading assigned: Wouldn't Take Nothing for My Journey Now
- Key
- 250 (specific amount and no more)
- Words
- Encyclopedic analysis

Technical Reasoning Words
- Brief

Confluence Words
- First impression

The decoding reveals that this assignment requires a significant amount of Precision (a total of six terms or references), a strategic use of Sequence to summarize and bullet (three references), and a negligible but strategic amount of Technical Reasoning (one reference), and Confluence (one reference). How does your answer compare to the answer above?

Knowing the mental energy required to complete a specific task helps assuage the feeling that you are in uncharted waters. Using the tool of Decoding allows you to feel informed and prepared for the task at hand. Using the strategic tool of FITing completes the "gearing up" that is necessary to be prepared to take on uncharted waters.

The Strategic Tool of FITing

The purpose of this tool is to match the use of your Compass Rose of Directional Forces to the type and amount of Directional Forces required by the task. In other words, when you **FIT** your Learning Processes to an assignment, you can specifically match them to the task and in doing so provide the exact learning resource needed to accomplish the task efficiently and correctly.(**FIT is an acronym for Forge, Intensify, and Tether**) (See Table 5.1) The tool of FITing operates in the following manner:

- Once you have decoded the key words of the assignment and matched them to the Word Wall, you need to count how frequently the assignment directs you to use each of the Processes: Sequence; Precision; Technical Reasoning; and Confluence.
- Next compare the required degree of usage to your LCI scores.
- Does the required degree of usage match your Learning Processes? With what specific Processes do you have a sufficient amount? Where do you have an over-abundance? With which do you come up short? (This is important to note since you will be using this information to FIT (Forge, Intensify, and Tether) your Directional Forces to the assignment. In other words, this is where you become an intentional learner.
- As an intentional learner you pay attention to the amount of effort you need to invest in using each of your Processes to complete each specific portion of the task!

Knowing when and how to match your Directional Forces to an assignment helps you plan for success by focusing on what you are required to do with your Learning Processes.

MY DIRECTIONAL FORCES	THE TASK	THE DIFFERENCE BETWEEN MY DIRECTIONAL FORCES AND THE TASK	REQUIRED ACTION: FORGE, INTENSIFY, OR TETHER
SEQUENCE I avoid (09)	Chronological, organize, record, average, trend (connect data points)	I definitely need to use much more Sequence than I naturally have.	I will need to **Forge my Sequence** in order to get this task done!
PRECISION I use this as needed (21)	Record, identify, and explain.	I need to use more Precision, but I should be able to do this if I just keep my Precision alert.	I will **wake up my Precision** and Use It As Needed to a higher degree. I will make my explanation of the trend longer than just two sentences.
TECHNICAL REASONING I use this as needed but at the lower end of the range (19)	Explain the trend reads like I just need to use words to explain, but I think when I connect the data points, I am actually building the slope of the trend, and that means I am using my Technical Reasoning.	I have enough Technical Reasoning to solve this problem.	**I will not need to take any special action** in order to use my Technical Reasoning on this assignment.
CONFLUENCE This is my Use First (33) Directional Force. It always wants to jump into an assignment and play with it or change it.	There is *no* Confluence required!	I want to use my Confluence, but this task requires none.	**I will need to Tether my Confluence** and not let it get in my way.

Table 5.1: Knowing when and how to match your Directional Forces to an assignment helps you plan for success by focusing on what you are required to do with your Learning Processes.

The tool of FITing consists of three lines of attack: Forge, Intensify, and Tether. Delve into the descriptions that follow and consider how each aspect of FITing can be used to complete the learning assignment you face in college, on the job, or at home.

Forge

The term **Forge** is applied to those Directional Forces that fall between 7 and 17 on the Learning Connections Inventory (LCI) Scoring Scale. The purpose of Forging a Directional Force is to increase its use and performance. Impossible? No. Does it require your attention and intention? Absolutely! It also requires an increased use of mental energy.

Regardless of which Process you need to Forge or how many Processes you Avoid, the amount of mental energy you need to alter a Directional Force's natural level of performance is directly related to the degree to which you Avoid it. For example, my LCI score in Sequence is 9. I Avoid Sequence to a great degree. To Forge this, I need to employ an extraordinary amount of energy to move it to a greater level of proficiency. I also need to recognize that this state of Forging has its limits. I can only Forge for an additional five points (9 + 5 = 14), which leaves me still in the Avoid category (but better!), and I can only sustain that intensity of energy for a brief period—a few minutes, several hours, possibly two or three days. Then the Directional Force will return to its natural level of use.

Keep in mind that when you are required to Forge an Avoid Process for a significant period, you will not have the same amount of energy to devote to coping with your other Learning Processes. Take, for instance, the following task:

> Submit a **chronologically organized list** of the assignments you have completed for this course. Record your grade for each assignment, **averaging** your initial grade with the grade earned for the last submission. **Identify and explain any trends that you observe.**

When I read words that call for the use of Sequence (chronological, list, organize), I immediately sense that I am being asked to enter uncharted waters. I know that if I am to succeed, I need to explore carefully what I am being asked to do, and then identify what personal strategies I will engage to navigate my way through the task. (See a list of strategies relating to each Directional Force of your Compass Rose in Appendix B.)

Intensify

The term **Intensify** refers to heightening the intensity with which you engage a Use As Needed Directional Force in order to accomplish a specific task. Intensify is always directed at those Use As Needed Patterns which fall within the 18-24 range of the LCI Scale Scores. These are the Patterns of your Compass Rose that often are mistaken as inactive. If you do not Intensify its use, it will remain quietly in the background unnoticed and underused. If your Directional Force operates closer to the Avoid edge of the Use As Needed continuum, then it remains almost dormant unless awakened. On the other hand, if it operates at the upper edge of the Use As Needed continuum, then it is more actively and readily available for use without a great deal of attention having to be paid to it.

The interesting thing about the Processes we Use As Needed is that they provide a rich set of options for us. These Directional Forces are neither our high-maintenance Processes nor our anchors that tend to weigh us down. They, instead, serve as our ballast, providing a counterbalance, ballast to the extremes of our Use First and Avoid Processes.

I have two Use As Needed Patterns in my Compass Rose: Precision and Technical Reasoning. In the case of the "itemized list of expenditures in chronological order" portion of the task, I can use my Technical Reasoning (19) from a practical business perspective to see the value in having these data available.

Further, I can take heart that I am not being asked to "write a report that identifies and analyses the similarities and differences between the two years of expenditures." Listing means fewer words; using fewer words suits my 21 in Precision just fine. Will I need to increase the use of my Precision a bit to have all the expenditures listed accurately? Yes. But the use of the mental energy I need to do so is nowhere near as exhausting as that required to do this task solely by using my Avoid Sequence Process. My Use As Needed Processes give me respite from the pain of trying to accomplish this task with Sequence alone. They calm my Sequence and coach my Use First Confluence to look for calmer seas.

Tether

The term **Tether** is applied to those Directional Forces you Use First. These fall into the 25 to 35 LCI Scale Score range. These noisy Processes drive your life and your learning. They dominate the makeup of your Compass Rose and always seek to be in charge of your destiny. Not infrequently, people will ask me if it is better to have more or fewer Use First Directional Forces. My response is, "You have what you have." As your Directional Forces formed randomly in your brain-mind interface, some became the dominant lead Processes while others assumed the roles of Use As Needed and Avoid.

Whatever your makeup, you sail through life with the Compass that formed, and if that Compass consists of one, two, three, or more Use First Learning Processes, then the Directional Forces that drive your life and learning are just what you need. All you are required to do is to learn to make them work for you. Of course, the challenge of using a combination of Use First Processes in concert with your Avoid and Use As Needed Processes is to do so with intention. In the case of your Use First Processes, the intention is to be on alert for when these more vocal Directional Forces need to be Tethered, that is, pulled back, held down, and restrained from overpowering the sails you have carefully set. Yes, there is such a thing as too much wind in your sails.

> *My learning ability is my own. It must be used thoughtfully so that I can continue to do well in whatever field I attempt.*

Tethering involves addressing those Directional Forces that want to hold sway regardless of the course set or the winds encountered. Often, it is our Use First Processes that bring us out of port self-assured, believing that it will be a smooth sail. Then, when we encounter adversity, it is these same Processes that want to stay the course, even when our Use As Needed Directional Forces are urging caution and midcourse correction.

Our Use First Processes announce our confidence. The difficulty is that these Processes do not represent competence. Their confidence is sometimes misplaced! Thus, Tethering them helps us gain perspective by communicating with our entire Compass Rose. This is truly a sign of our maturity and our mastery of the skills to navigate our life successfully.

For example, if we can return again to the case of the itemized list of expenditures and apply the tool of Tethering, I find that in my case, where my Use First Process is Confluence at a level of 33, I would naturally ignore the required list-and-compare requirement, writing it off in my mind as a dull way to identify the change that has or has not occurred. Left un-tethered, my Confluence would then lead me to compare one or two of the major expenditures but not all and would represent the comparison in a figurative rather than literal form. Because either approach would fall short of the expectations for the assignment, I might be perceived as a fool, a slacker, or an incompetent.

Because none of these are what I want to be seen as by my colleagues, I will Tether my Confluence, develop a comparative chart, run it by someone with higher Precision and Sequence than I, and then, having made their suggested changes, submit the report in a timely fashion.

Never Underestimate the Costs

FITing your Directional Forces to an assignment can cause a major energy drain. The task at hand must be carefully and accurately Decoded. The amount of resources needed to accomplish it needs to be carefully assessed. Never discount the Directional Forces needed to accomplish the task. Give yourself the space emotionally, mentally, and physically to FIT your Compass Rose to the task. Build in opportunities to re- generate your energy if you have been Tethering or Forging your Compass Patterns for hours at a time. Yet even taking into consideration the amount of energy required to Decode and FIT the task before you, never underestimate the tremendous feeling of accomplishment that awaits you when you have succeeded in completing an assignment to a degree that you have not achieved before. And never leave port without the knowledge of these three tools: Forge, Intensify, and Tether. They are the rudders that make it possible for you to navigate uncharted waters.

Staying the Course in Uncharted Waters

Knowing your Compass Rose equips you with the tools and the responsibility to overcome the fear of uncharted waters. Using your Compass Rose and your knowledge of how to **Decode** and **FIT** your Learning Processes, readies you to push back the fear and concerns that lie in uncharted waters.

- Don't let the situation control you.
- Don't let fear control you.
- Don't arrive under-resourced.
- Don't arrive without Personal Strategies.

The most efficient way to do this is to develop a personal Strategy Card. (See Figure 5.4.) This is the nitty-gritty of directing your learning behaviors. This is what guides your self-regulation and converts your good intentions into meaningful actions that yield the result you are seeking (Marzano, 1992).

A strategy card helps you organize your learning logic. It brings all the pieces of the assignment into the open. It frames the task, fills in the details, and provides a series of steps that will lead to success in completing the task. The strategy card is a carefully organized chart consisting of five levels.

Level 1: This is the line on which to record the scores of your four Directional Forces:

Level 2: These boxes provide space to record a brief description of you as a learner (refer to your Personal Learning Profile).

Level 3: This line allows you to categorize and record the key words of the assignment, matching them to the words found on the Word Wall.

Level 4: These are the boxes in which to label the action required to FIT your efforts to the Task (Forge, Intensify, Tether).

Level 5: These boxes broad space to record specific strategies of how you will use your Learning Processes with intention to accomplish the task.

In bulleted form, write a brief definition of critical thinking.

DAN	SEQUENCE	PRECISION	TECHNICAL REASONING	CONFLUENCE
Place your LCI scores in the boxes provided	25	18	30	14
Place a Description of your Learning Patterns in the boxes below. Use Your Personal Learning Profile to help guide the writing of your Pattern descriptions.				
How do you "naturally" use each of your Learning Patterns?	I need clear directions. Just tell me what you want me to do. I make bulleted lists. They are clear and direct.	I don't like to write. Words don't come easily.	I like to fix things. I can problem solve well. I like to work by myself. I don't ask for help ever.	It's hard for me to come up with ideas. I don't like to guess the meaning of what someone is saying or writing. I want it in black and white.
In the space provided below, describe the degree to which the assignment is asking you to use each Pattern to complete it. Use your decoded assignment to guide your completion of the boxes.				
What does the assignment require each of your Learning Patterns to do?	Bulleted format	Write definition of critical thinking	Brief	NOTHING REQUIRED
In the space provided below, list the strategies you will use to help you Forge, Intensify, and Tether your Learning Patterns so you can complete the assignment efficiently and effectively.				
How can you Forge, Intensify, or Tether your Learning Patterns to complete the task successfully?	This matches me. I don't need to use a strategy to FIT this. I can do it naturally.	Help! Start with something I know how to do. I can take things apart and see how they work. I can take Critical Thinking apart and break it down into parts. I can name the parts and see how each functions when a person is doing critical thinking. Then I can reassemble the parts of critical thinking and make a list of them and describe what each does.	I can keep things brief! No need to strategize here.	NOTHING REQUIRED

Figure 5.4: The purpose of Dan's strategy card is to fit him to the assignment. Using a strategy card will do the same for you.

You are more effective when you develop a Strategy Card for each major assignment. You are even more effective when you complete a logistical analysis and a strategic plan based on your FIT review. In doing so, you become more disciplined to put forth intentional, focused effort. At that point, the uncharted seas are nowhere near as formidable.

Strategy Card
Tracy Encizo

There is no single correct format for a strategy card. Over time you can learn to develop a strategy card format that works most effectively for you.

TASK: Figure out internship tasks: research best practices in three key areas, reach out to other agencies and compile critical information that can be applied to Phoenix property, track contacts, gather academic sources and create customized database and system of annotated bibliographies, collect practical and academic sources and sort into an index.

SEQUENCE	PRECISION	TECHNICAL REASONING	CONFLUENCE
29 (Use First)	25 (Use First)	22 (Use as Needed)	18 (Use as Needed)

organize
sort
classify
label
sequence
list
collect
	identify
	compare
	relevant
	document
	information
	research
	contrast
		figure out
		problem solve
		build
		track
			create
			brainstorm
			risk
			dive
			reach out to strangers,
			  unknown situations, new
			  areas of knowledge

Organize tasks into a sequence of steps and prioritize. Create master contact list, list of 25 possible academic sources, and list of local agencies.	Identify most relevant examples, practices, policies. Document available services.	Figure out relationships, problem solve barriers, build a portfolio. Be aware of demographics, geological considerations.	Brainstorm sources of info. Dive right in. Risk exposure. Create relationships.
TETHER	INTENSIFY	FORGE	FORGE
1. Don't get caught up in the organizational structure at this point. 2. Just get going on the work!	1. Look for relevancy, document findings, gather appropriate information, research, research, research. 2. Don't be in a hurry, but be thorough and take good notes. But don't get bogged down in minutiae.	1. I will solve whatever problems arise. Some things I can't know but I can do this project and get results. 2. Ask the director when encountering something far out of my area.	1. Risk instead of worrying about not having all of the answers when talking to contacts. 2. Reach out, ask questions, and keep track of what I need to find out to take the project further.

Figure 5.5: There is no single correct format for a strategy card.
Over time you can learn to develop a strategy card format that works most effectively for you.

Recording the strategies you used to achieve success disciplines you to put forth intentional, focused effort. College students can employ these navigational tools to chart their responses to course assignments within days of identifying their Directional Learning Forces.

When we know what comprises the Directional Forces of our Compass Rose, and when we are able to articulate how these Forces operate within us, then we have a language by which we can articulate our concerns, analyze specific tasks, identify specific problem-solving strategies, and achieve a successful outcome-even in the face of uncharted waters.

> Developing a Strategy Card requires you to invest, not avoid; dig deeper, not skim the surface of the task at hand.

Boxing the Compass

- The Directional Forces of your Compass Rose allow you to Decode, analyze, and perform in uncharted water.
- The use of personalized learning strategies allows you to navigate uncharted waters by positioning your Compass Rose to stay the course.

Taking Stock

1) Choose an upcoming task that might be difficult for you. Use the tool of Decoding and the Word Wall (See Figure 5.3.) to analyze the task. Examine how understanding your Directional Forces of Learning Processes helps you better understand and plan for the task.

2) Think about a time when you were less successful in completing an assignment than you wanted to be. How could you have used the strategic tool of FITing to have more successfully completed the task?

3) Select an upcoming assignment that is important to you. Using your knowledge of your Compass Rose, develop a personal Directional Forces Strategy Card. (Study Figures 5.4 and 5.5 to guide you in completing your own personal Strategy Card (See Worksheet 5.1.).

4) To see an example of how the Learning Tools of decoding and FITing can be used in the college classroom, turn to Appendix C and review how a professor uses these tools to heighten his students' opportunity to succeed in the uncharted water of physics.

Practice Strategy Card

	SEQUENCE	PRECISION	TECHNICAL REASONING	CONFLUENCE
Place your LCI scores in the boxes provided				
Place a Description of your Learning Patterns in the boxes below. Use Your Personal Learning Profile to help guide the writing of your Pattern descriptions.				
How do you "naturally" use each of your Learning Patterns?				
In the space provided below, describe the degree to which the assignment is asking you to use each Pattern to complete it. Use your decoded assignment to guide your completion of the boxes.				
What does the assignment require each of your Learning Patterns to do?				
In the space provided below, list the strategies you will use to help you Forge, Intensify, and Tether your Learning Patterns so you can complete the assignment efficiently and effectively.				
How can you Forge, Intensify, or Tether your Learning Patterns to complete the task successfully?				

Worksheet 5.1: Strategy Card (formatted) Blank

PART II
Finding Your Way: Setting the Course

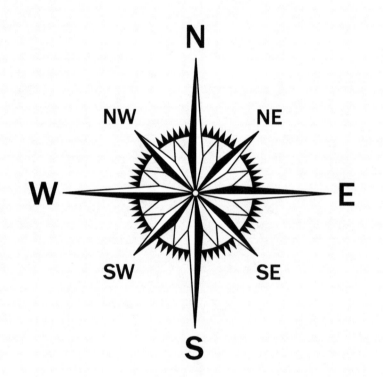

VI. NAVIGATING THE LEARNING CHALLENGES OF YOUR LIFE

"There are no secrets to success. It is the result
of preparation, hard work, and learning from failure."
—Colin Powell

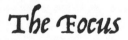

The Focus

• *Learning to take responsibility for navigating your life*
• *Detaching anchors that weigh you down*

Navigating life is not easy sailing. It is a daily, daunting task. As you prepare to plot your life with your new self awareness as a learner, you will want to do some final preparations. Begin by first checking the following:

- Have you identified your True North and begun to chart your course to achieve it?
- Are you aware of potential that lies within your Compass Rose?
- Are all metacognitive hands on deck?
- Can you use your Directional Forces and personal learning tools in concert?

If the answer to each of these questions is "yes," then you are almost ready to weigh anchor. One critical action needs to occur first, and that is making certain you are prepared to detach from old behaviors and execute your awareness of yourself as a learner. Are you able to stay in the moment and base your actions not on the way you have always done it, but on your awareness of your Compass Rose, and the potential it holds?

Most important, are you ready to allow your Compass Rose to direct you and your metacognition to transcend your old behaviors? Many times when we embark on a new venture, we take our old habits, behaviors, and personal learning history with us-even when we want to change. Be aware that knowing your Compass Rose and using it with intention will not remove life's obstacles. There will be an initial discomfort as you learn to use your Compass Rose with intention, a temporary lag in action as you learn to FIT your Directional Forces to the task and communicate with your metacognitive crew. It will feel different at first. However, the benefits gained from knowing your Compass Rose far outweigh the temporary discomfort as you transition into being a more effective learner.

> *The intentional use of your Compass Rose helps you go far beyond the surface of your personality to the heart of your human essence—your learning self.*

Weighing Anchor

Personal anchors affect our ability to maneuver and navigate our lives! They slow down our change process, and they weigh on our minds. If not confronted and removed, they can inhibit the successful navigation of our lives. The story that follows illustrates this point.

The Stories

Story I: Bob (Dr. Robert Grandin)

Sequence 22   Precision 26   Technical Reasoning 28   Confluence 30

I met Bob in Greece. We were both attending an international conference on learning and instruction. He came to my presentation on Learning Processes and approached me immediately afterward. "This is what I have been doing with students at my school," he said. "But I've had no language, no terms by which to call it. This is fabulous, just fabulous." And so began the tale of my journey with Bob.

Now, from the outset, it is important for the reader to know that I have Bob's permission to tell this tale, and I remain a colleague of Bob's even though thousands of miles separate us. I share his story because it is one of a person vested in knowing and understanding his Compass Rose, but choosing not to use it to live by.

Bob hails from Australia. He is a nationally recognized hero of the Battle of Long Tan (South Vietnam), a decorated Air Force helicopter pilot in Vietnam, a math teacher, an author, a sheep rancher, a cattle farmer, a school administrator, a shop owner, a consultant, a university instructor, and a husband, father, and grandfather. (The last, I believe, is the highest source of his pride.)

Bob is a Strong-willed Learner. He uses three Use First Directional Forces to lead his life. He avoids none. He is a force to be reckoned with. For over 65 years, Bob has intuitively navigated his life journey using his Use First Precision, Use First Technical Reasoning, and Use First Confluence. Bob is a dyed-in-the-wool one-man team.

He has had his successes in life and his failures. He would attribute both to his Strong-willed use of his Compass Rose. Bob's True North involves freeing himself and others to experience the fullness of life without the labels and limitations placed by traditional education. He is committed to making a difference to that end. He is determined to grow further in one area: developing the navigational skills and the discipline to FIT his Processes to those with whom he is working when the situation calls for it.

At my invitation, Bob came to the United States and worked with me at our Let Me Learn, Inc. national center. During that time, he provided services to teachers of adjudicated youth, intervention teams at a large center for early childhood education, and teachers in a secondary regional school system. Bob found following office and university procedures somewhat taxing. As a result, he simply ignored them. He did not take responsibility for his Use As Needed Sequence to follow procedures, but instead made up his own rules.

At one point during an annual performance review, he turned to me, his supervisor, and ten years his junior, and said, "Mate, are you concerned that I don't follow your directions?"

I responded, "I'm concerned that you think you are following the directions you choose to follow, but you ignore the others and are so certain of yourself that you don't check with others to see if you are on the right course. You don't self regulate. Instead you let your Strong-willedness get in the way of doing what is expected of you."

Bob countered, "Let me explain something to you. I ran away and joined the Australian Air Force when I was 16. My commanding officer had me in his office for a talk, and it wasn't because he wanted to commend me. He delivered his message, made his point as to why I was in his presence, and then concluded, 'Robert, apparently you believe there is only one job in this nation that suits you.'"

Bob said, "I asked him, 'What might that be, sir?'"

'Prime Minister,' and then he added without blinking, 'and that spot is already taken!'

At that point, Bob turned to me and said, "Don't worry if you haven't gotten me to change. It's been over 50 years since I first heard those words. I think they probably still ring true."

So why is Bob "the first story" of this chapter? Bob is an example of someone who lives his life to the fullest, holding fast to the skills he learned as a young man playing rugby: fake, trick, dodge, and weave. He holds fast to these anchors and they to him. After all his time teaching others the Let Me Learn Process, Bob has never embraced using his Compass Rose and knowledge of his Directional Forces himself. Therefore he does not use them with intention to navigate his life. What Bob is still working to develop are personal strategies that can help him address his Strong-willedness and assuage his Confluent tendencies to live life as an all-or-nothing wager, regardless of its impact on those around him.

The Learning: Bob's Story

As I reflect on Bob's story, I recognize that of all the aspects of the Let Me Learn Process Bob knew, developing strategies to reconfigure the use of his Directional Forces for specific tasks or assignments was the least appealing to him. I think, however, at this point, it is important to reveal that when I approached Bob about using his story to illustrate the challenge of ridding ourselves of habits that anchor us down and affect our willingness to change, he graciously consented stating:

"It is always difficult to read things that cut close to the bone. I do recognize that this is my Achilles' heel. I can only explain that as a Strong-willed Learner when you see a solution immediately, you often do not listen to the way others see the solution. I hope that by telling my story it helps others to recognize the point that understanding your Learning Patterns, or Compass Rose, as you call it, can help each of us be more productive in learning and working with others."

> *The requirements for finding your way involve engagement, execution, discipline, and detachment.*

There is no doubt. The requirements for finding your way involve engagement, execution, discipline, and detachment. Finding your way demands a commitment to begin the separation from old behaviors (our frailties of habit); and a significant degree of willingness to change when we find ourselves off-course.

Story II: David's

| Sequence 19 | Precision 26 | Technical Reasoning 28 | Confluence 20 |

David's parents and elementary-school teachers described him as a lazy student and an underachiever who was bright, but not living up to expectations. High school was no different. Because he was expected to go to college, he did, but he did not succeed, and after one semester, dropped out. For several years, he worked different jobs and traveled. The high point of his time away from college was when he used his self-taught instructional technology (IT) skills to develop a project for an overseas charter school. However, that was a small and fleeting success. Meanwhile, David's friends completed college and moved on with their lives.

David continued to struggle with his self-image as an underachiever. He felt restless and dissatisfied. He knew that he had walked away from a key part of his life. It haunted him, and at the same time, it terrified him. What would happen if he returned to college and failed again?

Ultimately, David chose to return to college because he wanted the challenge—but more than that, he wanted to redeem his sense of self as a learner. He wanted to overcome the negative thoughts, actions, and feelings from his prior experience. As an adult, he no longer was concerned solely with pleasing others; he sought personal fulfillment. He viewed his potential for success as a means of gaining self-confidence and self-worth. Unlike Bob in the previous story, David was willing to face himself and began to take his first steps towards becoming an intentional learner.

However, without understanding himself as a learner, David soon took on his old habits of not completing assignments and not communicating with either his instructors or his peers. Within weeks, he was back where he started—failing and seeing his dreams of success fading fast. When a friend suggested he find a learning coach, David jumped at the idea. During his very first session, his coach helped him identify his Directional Forces and how to make them work for him instead of against him. David began to understand how the mental processes within his Learning Processes interacted, creating within him a poor sense of self as a learner. He quickly recognized the effect his Directional Forces had upon his academic performance.

The insights David learned about himself included:

- Why he found it difficult to follow someone else's directions. Even when something didn't make sense to him, he wouldn't ask for clarification because he wanted to appear self-sufficient;
- Why if his work didn't meet his high, self-imposed standards, he didn't turn it in; and
- Why he wanted to work alone and not have to depend on others.(In fact, he preferred not sharing his work product with others, feeling it was important only to work to his standards.)

As a result of his combination of Directional Forces, David had never reached out for help, didn't believe in submitting drafts of papers, and didn't receive the coaching and mentoring from peers and instructors that could have made all the difference. David also was not very willing to try new approaches so talking to a learning coach about his frustrations was taking a big risk on his part.

Yet as soon as his coach helped him connect with his Learning Processes and their thoughts, feelings, and actions, David began to confront his fear of failure. He explained, "This has actually been something I've wrestled with all my life—this huge burden of pride and expectation. I want to succeed. I believe I can. Then I don't succeed, and I think I'm a fraud."

David had anticipated when he reached out for help that he would hear what he had always experienced from teachers and adult instructors before. Instead, the exchange revolved around:

- How the brain-mind connection and memory work.
- How to listen to the chatter within his mind and externalize his internal talk of fear, fraud, and prior negative experiences.
- How to face his feelings; identify their source; and take action to restore self-acceptance.

A few weeks after learning about his Learning Processes, David emailed his learning coach,
"I don't know what things would have looked like now if I hadn't met with you; the little we shared
really helped turn around a lot of my thinking and the course of perhaps my academic career."

His courses that semester ended with all papers completed, all tests taken, and a required poster presentation given.

The Learning: David's Story

David provided his own analysis of what he had learned from this part of his journey: "I had to remind myself not to be afraid. I didn't have to be afraid of receiving feedback or of having my work critiqued. By turning in my work and welcoming the feedback, I was able to break through the fear of making mistakes and not always being correct."

David's fear of failure is directly attributable to his Use First Precision which never wanted to make a mistake and his Use First Technical Reasoning which never wanted to show any weakness by asking for help.

When asked how he had turned the semester around, David said he had confronted his Precision and its chatter of, "You might make a mistake, so don't even try," and the message of his Technical Reasoning, "don't appear less than capable. Tough it out," and worked to tether both. Also, he made a conscious effort to communicate with each of his instructors (something he never would have done before). "Then I took their suggestions on papers and projects and I came up with some way to make it work. I took it in a direction that was doable for me. I did my own type of research. And I turned in my final anthropology paper on time!"

"Once I exorcised my learning demons, I was willing and able to make learning work for me. And within a matter of weeks, and with real effort, I succeeded."

It is in David's final sentence that we see the real difference between the stories of Bob and David. Bob clung to his known and comfortable behaviors, while David chose to use the new awareness of himself as a learner and to act upon it!

Just as in David's case, you can also use the knowledge of your Directional Forces to understand how to achieve your goals with greater awareness and intention. Like David, you can chart your path to success not just in college, but also in the workplace and in your personal life. That's exactly what David did. It has been eight years since I first met with David. He finished both his undergraduate and graduate degrees-having taken the opportunity to follow his True North-and is currently working as a counselor to ex-offenders who are seeking to find their way.

The Anchors that Affect Our Personal and Professional Lives

The Drivers

One of the most insidious of anchors is the "Drivers," a concept first developed by Dr. Tabai Kahler who suggested that from early childhood we are taught five little messages (mini-scripts) that stay with us all of our lives (Kahler, 1977).

- Be Perfect!
- Please Me!
- Try Hard!
- Be Strong!
- Hurry Up!

Initially spoken by our parents as a set of rules for ordering our lives, these mini-messages grow to be the Drivers of our behavior. Once we enter formal schooling as learners, the message of these mini-scripts is reinforced daily.

In school the Be Perfect message becomes, "Don't turn in work with any mistakes. Correct your errors. No erasures. No smudges. No coloring outside the lines." Once in the classroom the Please Me message morphs from a parent's raised voice to the teacher's raised eyebrow which conveys, "You are not pleasing me. Stop whatever it is you are doing, and start to do what I say. That is the only thing that pleases me." The "Try Hard" measure becomes a mode for excusing yourself from taking responsibility for your lack of action or progress. You simply cover up your lack of engagement by saying, "I tried," only to hear the counter response, "Well not hard enough!"

The message of Be Strong is straight forward. Don't show on the outside what you are feeling on the inside. It makes you appear weak and less than capable. Come on and suck it up." And all the while you are being perfect by pleasing me, you need to show less emotion. No one has time to deal with your feelings so would you just be strong and hurry up? Your behaviors are slowing down the progress of life, so pick up the pace and let's move. I have places to go, people to see, things to do, and your behavior is slowing me down!"

These Drivers don't operate in isolation either. They like to cling to our Learning Processes and become a part of the chatter within and among our Directional Forces (See Table 6.1). Their messages are simple, powerful, and debilitating. You have only to look back at David's story to see it.

The internal chatter of our mind can become jumbled when our Directional Forces and Drivers fill our head with mixed messages.

The Driver	The Message of Your Drivers and the demands they place on you.	The Empowering Message that Disarms your Drivers and frees you from their impossible to meet demands.
Be Perfect	**I always seek to Be Perfect:** I am fastidious. I want my writing and speaking to be error free. I check and doublecheck whatever I say and write. Sometimes I write over words or repeat what I've said so that my message is perfectly clear. I use many adjectives and adverbs so that every little last detail can express precisely what I want it to perfectly. I almost always never make a mistake. I correct others when they make mistakes because it shows I value getting the details correct, well actually, perfect.	**I will do my very best:** Perfect is important for gemologists but not if I am engaging in learning. I learn, i.e., change, grow, and adapt from my mistakes. It is not possible to be perfect. It is important to have the opportunity to learn from my mistakes in a nonthreatening environment.
Please Me	**I always seek to Please Others** I like to do things the way I am supposed to because it pleases those in charge, usually, that is. I always ask lots of questions several times a week or maybe a day. There is no margin for error if I want to get on the good side of the instructor. I spend a lot of time figuring out how to anticipate what the instructor wants.	**I set reasonable goals that will meet my personal expectations of my professional performance.** If I choose to join an organization and buy into its purpose, then I will enjoy using my talents to achieve personal as well as organizational goals. It is under these circumstances that I will develop a healthy sense of professional personhood which will be recognized and respected by others.
Try Harder	**Make it seem as if you are Trying Hard even if you have no success.** I worry when I don't receive praise. Maybe I didn't try hard enough this time to do it right. But I did try. I spent a lot of time trying to complete that project to please both the board and him. I just can't win. Nothing is ever good enough.	**I will put forth measureable effort, and I make a difference.** Effort, unlike trying hard, is measurable, observable, and identifiable. It can be analyzed and used as a springboard for enhanced attention which leads to successful achievement of a goal. Trying hard is a shallow substitute.

Table 6.1a: Internal Chatter, Directional Forces and Drivers.

The Driver	The Message of Your Drivers and the demands they place on you.	The Empowering Message that Disarms your Drivers and frees you from their impossible to meet demands.
Hurry Up!	**I Hurry, Hurry and do things quickly and never stop, no matter the outcome.** I never have enough time to get things done. I'm always behind, swamped, stressed. For once, I'd like to meet a deadline without a hassle. I can't escape this rat race. That's what it is, just a rat race. Deadlines rule the day. Lists, schedules. I can't live without my daily planner or digital calendar.	**I am able to think, plan, and respond at a pace that allows me to develop and mature as a professional.** A professional requires time to plan, time to act, and time to reflect. Incubation and maturation take time. They cannot be hurried. Development has its own timetable.
Be Strong	**I need to Be Strong because Everything depends on me.** I'm a real take-charge person. I'm strong. I don't let emotions or time rule me. I control them. If I can get people to follow my directions perfectly, then things work out well, and I become even stronger in the eyes of those I want to please.	**I am allowed to show emotions appropriate to a given situation.** The single source of strength for the professional is locus of control. If I can appreciate me for both my strengths and weaknesses, then I can accept both successes and failures and not need to hide my emotions behind a facade of impenetrable strength.

Table 6.1b: The internal chatter of our mind can become jumbled when our Drivers fill our head with mixed messages.

Drivers erode our sense of confidence while building self-doubt. They weigh us down! And because they have been with us, embedded by well-meaning parents, teachers, and other authority figures, we hesitate to challenge their veracity and validity. Only when we confront their presence in our lives, however, can we rid ourselves of their negative effect. Not only do we need to remove the Drivers, we need to replace them with a healthy message that supports and encourages us as learners.

When we convert the chatter of Please Me to the message, "It is important that I find satisfaction and take pride in the way I'm completing this assignment," we are taking the first step to owning our learning, owning our behavior, and affirming ourselves as likeable and capable learners. The same is true for the remaining messages. With intention we can hear the harmful chatter of Be Perfect and change it to, "I am committed to doing the best I am able to do. I will strive to achieve, knowing that 'No one is perfect.' I will learn from my mistakes, and in doing so strengthen my ability to take in the world around me, make sense of it, and respond appropriately."

Not needing to fake the effort you're putting forth, you no longer need the excuse, "Well I tried," but are declaring that you have made a "measurable effort," and will commit to using your metacognitive team of Directional Forces to "assess, reflect, and revisit" in order to improve your learning outcomes.

When confronting the effects of the Drivers within us, the Be Strong anchor becomes "I do not need to hide behind a façade of strength. I can reveal who I am as a learner and grow by asking for help or connecting to my fellow learners. I can strive to interact with my classmates so that I can 'learn together, perform alone,' the true essence of cooperative learning. And finally, "I no longer need to buy into the urgency of the Hurry Up Driver. Knowing myself as a learner, allows me to FIT my Learning Processes and pace myself. Slowing my pace allows me to Mull, Connect, Rehearse, Attend…well you understand. In other words when I say, "No!" to the Hurry Up Driver, I am protecting my space and pace, and I then have the time to invest in real and deep learning.

As you read further, notice how the Driver anchors insinuate themselves into the genetic code of the others. Only with intention can you eradicate the negative effects of the anchors upon your learning behaviors!

The Ever Ready Excuse

The Excuse thrives in an environment in which persons use their Compass Roses to make excuses for their behavior. They do not invest energy in listening carefully, following directions, or completing tasks as assigned. The Compass Rose of their Directional Forces becomes an excuse for noncompliance and slipshod work. They may say, "Oh, you know I don't understand directions. Just look at my level of Sequence. It's a glaring Avoid!"

Once you rid yourself of excuses, you recognize that knowing your Directional Forces provides you with an explanation of how you learn, but it does not provide you with an excuse for not changing your learning behaviors.

Your Directional Forces are an explanation, not an excuse!

> *Your Directional Forces are an explanation, not an excuse!*

Regardless of what constitutes your Compass Rose, you are responsible for using it to make life work. The point of Finding Your Way is just that! Know your True North, understand your Compass Rose, and make life work for you because you are now well equipped to do so.

The SMTDSLT Anchor

A particularly heavy anchor is the SMTDSLT (pronounced Smitd-Slit) standing for "So much to do; so little time." It operates like this within your life:

> *Navigating life is a great concept, and it is very intriguing, but I don't have time for visiting my Personal Learning Journey right now. Once I have this important project done, then I can consider visiting my Learning Journey and developing my Personal Compass Rose. Until then, I just need to keep doing what I am doing the best I know how. Later I can take time for myself. Right now, I have work, family, schedules, obligations, responsibilities.*

The SMTDSLT anchor literally brings people to a standstill and holds them captive with to-do lists, text messages, e-mails, and phone messages. It subsumes all personal time and personal space. It keeps you overscheduled and overwhelmed. It is what one author calls, "CrazyBusy" (Hallowell, 2007).

To avoid this conundrum, you will need to consider how you can rid yourself of the SMDTSLT anchor.

- Begin by revisiting your navigational tools and making your Strategy Card to get through various time-crunch situations.
- Then use your logistics of Decoding and the strategic use of FITing your Directional Forces to complete the assignment efficiently.

One thing to note is that practicing the use of your navigational tools expands your ability to respond to all types of situations. Regular and intentional use of your Compass Rose helps you find your bearings and helps you navigate a course equipped with insights and understanding of yourself that go far beyond the surface to the heart of your human essence—your learning self.

Staying the Course: Taking the Helm

People who only use the knowledge of their Compass Rose at surface level significantly underestimate its power to enhance and develop their personal and professional selves. The fact that Bob shared this sentiment suggests that he might possibly, after 20 years, come to the awareness that significant power to navigate his life can be found in the Directional Forces and the very tools he earlier had dismissed.

David's story shows us a much more productive way to respond to insights about our learning selves. There are many stories like David's, many lives that have been set on course once individuals recognized their need to better understand how to "take in the world around them, make sense of it, and learn to respond appropriately."

Where ever we look we can see the difference that knowledge of how we learn has made a difference. Whether for an honor student at a Midwestern college, a Health Sciences student at Virginia Commonwealth, a transfer student at Arizona State, a nontraditional student returning to college online, or a recent graduate from a top tier state university, understanding themselves as learners has made a significant difference in their ability to navigate their learning lives successfully!

Assuming the Helm

Having set your course and configured your Compass Rose, you are now prepared to assume responsibility for the same-different person you were before. You will possess the same intelligences, the same interests, and the same idiosyncrasies as those you had before reading and interacting with *Finding Your Way*, but now you know how to navigate life more efficiently and effectively. You understand how to use your Directional Forces and your navigational tools. You are prepared for the personal and professional change in perspective and motivation that is about to occur within you. In many ways, your new knowledge allows you to feel unbounded. You are emancipated from the labels and judgments you have experienced along your life journey.

You are equipped to remove the unproductive behaviors that have weighed you down and are prepared to use your metacognitive team to overcome your individual frailties. You are ready to assume responsibility in a manner that you have not been prepared to do so before. You are prepared to set and stay the course!

Boxing the Compass

- As the person in charge of my learning vessel, I need to execute my new awareness while detaching from old behaviors.
- Assuming the helm requires me to ready myself for the sea change ahead.

Taking Stock

Confronting the Unknown

- Keep a brief, running record this week of how you are interacting with tasks or topics confronting you at work and at home. Pay particular attention to how you respond to your SMTDSLT anchor.
- Review the situational excuses listed below. Then identify how you could use your Compass Rose and the Navigational Tools of Decoding, FITing, and Personal Strategies to address each:
    - I am not prepared, equipped, or experienced enough to do anything about the situation.
    - I don't see why others are concerned about this situation, so why should I be concerned and waste my time and energy?
    - I don't have sufficient information to make a determination as to what to do.
    - I don't want to risk making a mistake and losing others' respect or friendship, or my professional/financial status.

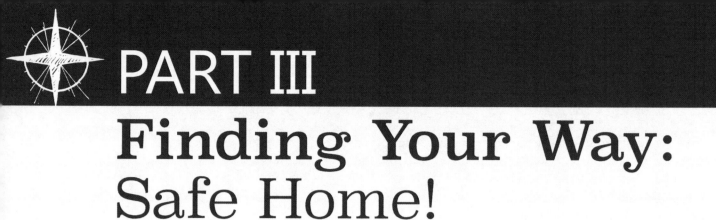

PART III
Finding Your Way: Safe Home!

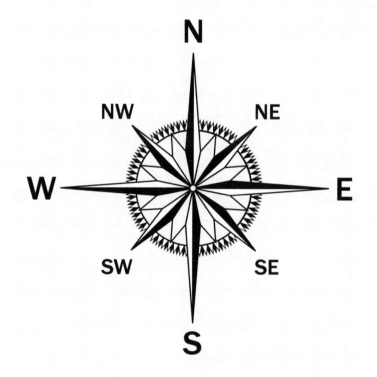

VII. NAVIGATING YOUR FUTURE

*The society that has…the ability to learn
will be the people who continue
to succeed and achieve*
—Thomas Friedman

The Focus

- Identifying the Critical Skills needed in the 21st century
- Understanding how the Directional Forces of your Compass Rose prepare you for success in college and career

Finding Your Way is a text about learning in the 21st century. As such, each chapter has explored the different and varied tools we need to meet the demands of the 21st century beginning with identifying the Directional Forces of our Personal Compass Rose. This final chapter emphasizes the central role they play in our ability to think critically, to read and write critically, and to make critical career choices (National Institute for Literacy, 2001). It is our Directional Forces of learning that provide the skill to navigate the world of the 21st Century. It is our Directional Forces that when harnessed to our True North serves the needs of all members of society in our fast paced technologically-driven world.

The Story

More than two decades ago, Neil Postman, a renowned media critic and author, warned us that with the advance of technology, we would soon be facing a virtual tsunami of information (Postman, 1990). He projected that this would result in a long-term negative effect on global society because *obtaining information faster does not ensure a more informed understanding of it or a wiser use of it*. He went further, suggesting that the missing element in dealing with the growth of information is the equal lack of growth in our ability to absorb, process, and respond to information at the same rate as its transmission.

Now, 20 years later, Postman's prophecy has come true. As a result of our access to information, our minds are swamped with words and data. Externally, our professional world inundates us with wave upon wave of information. We find ourselves sinking under its weight, unable to bail fast enough, to delegate and channel it quickly enough, and to keep ourselves afloat. The speed with which information is communicated leaves us with little time to establish its context, little time to process it, and even less time to discern its implications. Absorbing, digesting, and responding effectively under these circumstances is stressful at best and impossible at worst.

These are difficult seas we have to navigate and we need to ask ourselves: Can our minds absorb information at the pace it currently appears on our screens? Can we thoughtfully develop an understanding of the complicated and multifaceted challenges facing us? Can we learn to respond appropriately having weighed all the variables to a problem in the balance?

These are difficult seas we have to navigate and we need to ask ourselves: Can our minds absorb information at the pace it currently appears on our screens? Can we thoughtfully develop an understanding of the complicated and multifaceted challenges facing us? Can we learn to respond appropriately having weighed all the variables to a problem in the balance?

Thirteen years ago Neil Postman died not having written the ending to this story. We will write that ending in the years to come, and its conclusion will rely on a single factor: our ability to harness our minds to apply the skills of Critical Thinking, reading, writing, and decision-making to the ever-growing magnitude of information that confronts us.

> **Succeeding in the 21st century requires you to "take in the world around you (*use your brain and mind with intention*), make sense of it (*gain knowledge and develop learning tools*), and respond appropriately (*apply Critical Thinking, reading, writing, and decision-making to your personal, social, and professional lives*).**

The Learning Part I
The Critical Skills

While the term **critical** is frequently associated with criticism or blame, in the case of this chapter it refers to an intentional act by you to ask essential questions, to use reasoning, and to gather facts in order to arrive at an accurate, logical conclusion. You might liken critical skills to a type of mental gymnastics by which you strengthen and enhance your learning stamina. Table 7.1 frames the questions that are used to process in-coming information in each of the critical skills. As you read the table, note the tight relationship of Critical Thinking to Critical Reading, writing, and decision-making. As you move through the chapter you will see a table for each critical skill. The subsequent tables will differentiate each of the critical skills from the other, but here at the outset, they are presented as a unified group based on a common set of essential questions.

Common Factors of Critical Skills

	Critical Thinking	Critical Reading	Critical Writing	Critical Decision-making
Uses a rigorous process to expand knowledge, skills, and experience.	Asks complex questions.	Gathers relevant information.	Applies the rigorous process of pre-writing, writing, and editing to all written expression.	Gathers information from various sources to gain a broader perspective.
Seeks a broader understanding.	Poses an array of questions and analyzes essential data.	Reads for deep meaning.	Presents a broad spectrum of information from varied sources.	Asks essential questions.
Weighs information seeking to find a balance.	Refuses to settle for a surface understanding.	Reads an array of sources seeking to gain a balanced perspective.	Builds a case based on a variety or sources and references.	Seeks multiple sources representing various perspectives.
Makes a well reasoned case based on clear line of logic.	Communicates effectively with others in figuring out solutions to complex problems.	Seeks out models of research studies that provide a well-reasoned methodology.	Examines the writings of others to find a guide for developing a logical argument.	Identifies and notes the practical consequences resulting from each possible conclusion.
Tests logic for consistency.	Examines logic and reasoning when forming conclusions.	Tracks the line of logic by tracing a writer's progression of thought.	Identifies a composition's line of logic noting its step-by-step presentation.	Imitates the steps used by some held with respect for their well reasoned conclusions.
Explores new ways of viewing situations.	Thinks open-mindedly.	References a variety of sources and sees their over-arching connection.	Poses questions that invite responses from differing perspectives.	Exercises open-mindedness and willingness to try new never before tested ideas.

Table 7.1: Our critical skills of thinking, reading, writing, and decision-making share a common set of essential actions.

Critical Thinking

Critical Thinking does not occur by luck or by chance. You are not born a critical thinker. The skills and behaviors that produce Critical Thinking develop over time and through experience. Your Critical Thinking skills improve as you practice them. One way to begin their development is to identify which you consciously use, and which need greater attention and development. Table 7.2 will help you assess the degree to which you currently use your Critical Thinking skills.

As you read the list of statements, ask yourself: How frequently do I use any, some, or all of the strategies? Take note of the Learning Patterns required. Do your Learning Patterns match those that are required? If not, how might you use your combination of Learning Patterns to practice the skill? What strategies would you add to the chart?

Learning Patterns as they relate to Critical Thinking

Critical thinking skills	Pattern-based strategies to use
Take a position and defend it using logic.	Use Sequence to: • Establish a step-by-step line of reasonable thought. • Trace consistent pattern of thought.
Take a position and defend it using clarity, accuracy, precision, and depth.	Use Precision to: • Check the facts you have based your opinion on. • Recognize when what you are doing isn't increasing the quality of information you are seeking or resulting in a logical outcome.
Push the limits of your knowledge, reasoning, and logic.	Use Technical Reasoning to: • Examine the framework of your logic. • Use trial and error to test your logic. (Johnston, 2012)
Generate new ways of viewing situations outside the boundaries of the standard approach. (Paul, R., & Edler, L. (2001)	Use Confluence to: • Generate different ideas. • Accept failure and learn from it. • Determine reasonable alternatives.

Table 7.2: Our ability to use Critical Thinking Skills is greatly enhanced when we know which learning strategies best help us strengthen our thought processes.

Critical Reading

Critical Reading is not casual reading. It is not skimming an email or glancing at the headlines. It demands that you pay attention to the content of whatever you are reading including the "visual jargon" (the symbols, numbers, and graphs) found in the written directions, plans, manuals, and blueprints (Rose, 2004, p. 205). Critical Reading is not just for executives or nerds. Critical Reading is required when completing the most mundane of work tasks such as reading ingredient tables, spreadsheets, invoices, production quotas, shift logs, codes, and bills of lading.

Critical Reading is also **deep** or close reading. It engages you in *interpreting* text and *making rich mental connections* by picking up on contextual clues and making predictions based upon signs and evidence embedded in the text. Deep reading forces you to ask questions and then dig deeper to find the answers. It engages you in becoming a wordsmith and a detail detective. It motivates you to plumb the depths of the text you are reading. Table 7.3 provides a series of pre-reading questions that can help you prepare yourself to be a strong Critical Reader.

Key Questions for Critical Reading

What are you to know after reading the materials?	*What is being written about?* A story? A situation? An explanation of a real world phenomenon? An explanation of a process? **(Precision)**
	How does what you read unfold? From beginning to end? Through flashbacks? If you read about a science process or a history of something, what drives the process described in the reading? **(Sequence)**
	Who, what, where, and when? Why? **(Precision)** *How does it work? How was it formed? How does it operate? Are there diagrams to read and interpret? Graphics with labels? Numbers?* **(Technical Reasoning and Precision)**
	What is the central idea behind the passage? **(Confluence and Precision)** What new terms will you need to record, look up, and log for review? **(Sequence and Precision)**
How does the material prompt you to draw inferences and connect to existing knowledge?	*What did you learn from a previous reading assignment* that you can apply to this assignment? **(Sequence and Precision)** *What is being suggested or inferred,* but not actually stated in the material? **(Confluence)** *What information is implied* that you feel comfortable assuming is accurate because you have read something previously on a related topic? **(Sequence and Precision)** Johnston, 2012

Table 7.3: Asking yourself specific questions in advance of starting a reading assignment can help prepare your mind to read critically.

Your Directional Forces can help prepare your mind to think and read critically. A study of students' reading of textbook content at Arizona State University found the following:

- Students with **Use First Sequence** stated they always followed the same order when reading a textbook: Text, tables/charts, and then others (cartoons). Their eye tracking data confirmed this.
- Students with **Use First Precision** didn't finish all the pages because they didn't have enough time to read everything on the page, as they desired. When asked why they looked at what they looked at, they would over-explain in detail what they did and what they were thinking. They would also often explain more than just the written text, including the visuals.
- Students with **Use First Technical Reasoning** were very direct and to the point. They didn't spend much time in any of the ancillary (supporting) text. When they were asked to explain why they looked at what they did, their descriptions were very short. If asked to talk about a similar element, they replied, "The same as before." They also finished before the timed reading was up and did not review any material.
- Students with **Use First Confluence** looked at everything; most of the time they didn't finish reading the primary content unless it was interesting to them. When talking about what they read, they often spoke about what they felt and how it related to past experiences (Christopherson, 2012).

Critical Reading takes energy, an investment of time, and intention on your part. Why do it? Because so much of life requires you to be a critical reader—to not only understand what words mean but also what they don't mean. It means getting the message both from the words that appear on the page and from those that are implied. The feature box, "Tips to Improve Your Reading Comprehension," provides practical suggestions that will help you engage your Learning Processes to read for more than just basic comprehension.

Tips to Improve Your Reading Comprehension

- **Allow enough time to read through the material at least twice. Pick out the primary idea(s)** (*Precision*).

- **Find details that support the primary focus** (*Precision*).

- **Drill down for deeper meaning by using techniques that fit your Learning Patterns.**

- **For example, use a two-column format to identify the information or concepts that are clear after the first read-through and those that remain unclear** (*Sequence and Precision*).

- **Draw a graphic representation to depict how the new information connects to what you already know** (*Technical Reasoning and Confluence*).

- **Develop an information map that illustrates the logic of thought development from beginning to end of the reading. Add road signs to help you "slow down," "take caution," or be ready to stop and absorb particularly detailed or cognitively challenging information** (*Sequence, Precision, and Technical Reasoning.*)

- **Recognize how the material is organized** (*Sequence*).
    - **Headings and Subheadings**
    - **Questions**
    - **Glossaries**
    - **Charts, graphs, illustrations, and images**

- **Re-read difficult passages and say out loud what you think they mean. Draw a graphic representation—a web of ideas, a diagram, a chart, anything that works—illustrating your understanding of the passage** (*Technical Reasoning and Precision*).

- **Make up questions to quiz yourself or to ask the instructor or to post for peer responses** (*Confluence and Precision*).

Critical Writing

Critical Writing, like Critical Reading, relies on the development of intentional skills. What you write for college courses needs to be accurate, logical, carefully reasoned, and thoughtfully crafted. Critical Writing takes many forms (short answers, paragraph responses, postings, essays, research papers).

Regardless of the required format, gathering your thoughts from inside your mind and presenting them for public view can be the most challenging and, in some cases, the most agonizing of human acts. This is because writing, unlike reading, requires you to communicate your thoughts, experiences, and even innermost feelings using not pictures, not videos, not even your actual voice but scratches on paper or symbols on a screen that you hope have the same meaning to another person as you intended. Writing exposes you to others in a manner that no other human expression does (Johnston, 2005).

The main task of Critical Writing is to communicate from the inside out by having the mind convert its internal thoughts to external expression (Johnston, 2005).

Needless to say, Critical Writing is just as challenging a skill as Critical Reading. It requires your language processing muscles to be flexed regularly, so they are ready to do some heavy lifting to place words in a clear, logical, persuasive structure. It takes practice, and the more you do it, the better you get.

Developing your skill of Critical Writing begins by understanding how you learn—what directional forces you use to place your thoughts into words. Critical Writing, to be effective, also needs to be authentic, not formulaic. In other words, Critical Writing requires that you own your thoughts and the words you chose to express them. That is why preparing drafts, taking time to compose, set aside, re-read, and revise your written expression is so important. Neither texting nor tweeting promotes Critical Writing. Each relies on a quick response which often results in writer's remorse and the thought, "If only I could take back what I just sent." Critical Writing works with intention to achieve just the opposite.

> *The main task of Critical Writing is to communicate from the inside out by having the mind convert its internal thoughts to external expression.*

When developing your Critical Writing skills, it is sometimes helpful to read about the experiences of others, so you can identify how to apply their strategies to improve your writing. A common phrase used to describe this approach is "writer's workshop." Many colleges conduct writing labs for the same purpose—to encourage students to hone their Critical Writing skills by *rehearsing* them before *expressing* them (Here consider these terms in light of Chapter IV and the phases of the Metacognitive Drill.). What follows, therefore, in lieu of a table of Critical Writing strategies as found previously under Critical Thinking and Critical Reading, are the stories of four writers. Each of these individuals was introduced to you in Chapter III. You know their Directional Forces and how they see themselves as learners. Now engage in two specific actions: 1) Note how their combination of Directional Forces affects their approach to Critical Writing. Consider which of their Learning Processes supports the writing process and which might be detracting from it; 2) listen as they explain themselves as writers. Pay attention to the suggestions of their writing coach. See to whom you most relate. Then identify how you can develop your Critical Writing skills by learning from these writing experiences.

Sequence

Makayla, psychology major

Sequence 29   Precision 20   Technical Reasoning 17   Confluence 14

'Your paper is well executed but lacks originality.'

Makayla was ruled by her Sequence, almost to the point of paralysis. She spent hours taking notes, would drench her texts with hi-liter ink and produce step-by-step outlines for papers, but couldn't begin to draft if she didn't have the parts of her paper completed in order (intro, body, conclusion). Ultimately, she executed her papers well, but found that she received lower grades for "lack of originality" and being "unable to present any new or different" ideas.

Does this mean that people high in Sequence aren't creative? Absolutely not! It means that as a critical writer and as someone who understands her Directional Forces, Makayla can use personal learning strategies to Tether her Sequence to allow her to move beyond the specific directions and follow a less restrictive approach to completing the assignment. It means that with effort she can Forge her Confluence to find new ways to express her thoughts with greater verve and flair, occasionally taking a risk she wouldn't have dared before.

Precision

John, Lieutenant, US Army
Sequence 27   Precision 32   Technical Reasoning 21   Confluence 23
"TMI" (Too much information)

What's new?
These acronyms, for a start:
FOB- Forward Operating Base. Ok, I lied, this one's not new.
DFAC- Dining facility. Covered before, but to refresh your memories: a cafeteria (or dining facility)
BBK- Baraki Barak, the place where I live and wipe myself down with baby wipes instead of showering.

Not surprisingly, sometimes Precision can get a writer into trouble. If asked to write a 1500 word essay, a writer high in Precision often feels frustrated. "How am I supposed to fit all this into three pages? I didn't even get a chance to talk about XYZ!" While others may struggle to fill a page, a person high in Precision sees every detail as important, and sometimes feels it's impossible to cut what's been written.

Students who Use Precision First may feel a need to get everything that comes into their head onto paper. Then, they may have trouble eliminating details that aren't to the point. How did extreme Precision get our soldier into trouble? He seemed to lack a filter. He sent long, descriptive emails, chronicling every aspect of his days and nights-even the dangerous ones, wrenching the hearts of his loved ones. Simply TMI-too much information!

On the other hand, those who Avoid Precision frequently feel they have nothing to say, and may have trouble starting their first draft. After they have finished a draft, it may lack details or may contain grammar or spelling errors. And then comes a feeling of being lost or frustrated as they worry it's just not going to be good enough.

Technical Reasoning

Paul, engineering major
(Sequence 20,   Precision 16,   Technical Reasoning 33,   Confluence 24)
'Student of Too Few Words'

More and more, students who graduate with competence in their majors and who possess strong writing ability are the ones who get the jobs.

Even as you begin to read this scenario, you may be asking yourself, "What do scientists need to know about writing? Why make them take a writing course?"

Interestingly it's the scientist who can write that employers seek. In order to get new business, science and engineering companies need to write grants and proposals. They need to publish their findings, and they need employees who are able to communicate effectively with groups and individuals in writing.

More and more, students who graduate with competence in their majors and who possess strong writing ability are the ones who get the jobs.

For Paul the most effective strategy he needed to adopt was to identify the critical information needed to be incorporated into his project descriptions and then set the goal of writing three or four sentences about each key point. Next he needed to use his Sequence to put the points in the order of their importance and link the paragraphs together, splicing them with basic transition words such as first, next, then, or finally.

His grades were a wake-up call to him, and he sheepishly admitted that he hadn't bothered thoroughly reading the research he'd found in the library's databases but had skimmed through the abstracts. Paul blatantly ignored the very skills central to being a critical reader and writer.

By nature, those who use Technical Reasoning like Paul would rather "show" than "tell," but with an awareness of who you are as a learner and how you approach writing, you'll be better able to express yourself in writing. With practice, drafting, and editing, your writing skills will improve. Had Paul not received this counsel and used strategies that related to his Directional Forces, he would not have achieved success as a critical writer.

Confluence

Raheem, sociology major
(Sequence 11,   Precision 16,   Technical Reasoning 28,   Confluence 31)
"I plan to succeed by chance."

"I can be easily annoyed, but I don't worry very much. That's what makes me different." These two sentences constituted Raheem's entire first submission in his writing course. When questioned about its length and its philosophy (his idea of succeeding by chance), his response was,

"It's worked so far."

"Why such a short essay?" his instructor inquired.

"Pretty much sums it up," he replied.

Raheem dismissed his Patterns as "hocus pocus" and continued to rely on his idea of letting chance take care of him. His decision not to employ Critical Writing to his college assignments caught up to him. As more deadlines passed and the incompletes piled up, it became clear that he was not going to pass the course.

Do you identify with any of these writers or with portions of what they've said? How do you plan when you need to write something? Do you do everything you can to avoid putting your thoughts into words? Or do you look forward to expressing your thoughts in written form?

Critical Decision-making

The skill of Critical Decision-making is also essential to your success. It is central to finding and maintaining a career path. It will ultimately determine your economic future. These words are not just a rationale for pursuing a college degree; they reflect what a national coalition of business, commerce, labor, and educational leaders has identified as the four skills that most determine a person's economic success (Equipped for the Future [EFF] Standards, 2001, p. 17).

- Knowing how to take responsibility for learning;
- Knowing how to make informed decisions;
- Knowing how to communicate in speaking and writing; and
- Knowing how to solve problems (computational, mechanical, organizational, and personal).

Engaging in learning prepares your mind to develop life skills and strengthens your judgment and decision-making.

Adults who have these skills can build a bridge to the future. They can cope with a changing world and compete in a global economy. (The National Work Readiness Council's (NWRC), 2006; Ford, J., Knight, J., & McDonald-Littleton, E., 2001).

Engaging in learning prepares your mind to develop life skills and strengthens your judgment and decision-making.

As a student of the 21st-century who has come to an understanding of yourself as a learner, you are now ready to use your Critical Decision-making skills to connect your True North and your Compass Rose of Directional Forces to a career path (Johnston, 2010).

- You will want to begin this journey by re-visiting your True North. Then holding it as the guiding focus of your career exploration, begin to do a career exploration.
- Use any one of the online job hunting tools to assist you in your search. But before you began to go far afield in your search, stop and do a reality check. Look for real-time positions in that career.
- Use your Critical Reading to decode several job descriptions. Focus on what employers in that career expect, not just as entry level education requirements. What performance skills are required?

For example, let's say you are interested in a health science career. You have taken the basic science courses that would prepare you to enter any number of health careers after finishing your undergraduate degree. You recognize that you have many avenues from which to choose. Before you go further it is wise to take a reality check. After all, a career is more than just a job title.

> *I believe there are many steps to finding a career path. First comes the desire to make money by having a job. Then it's nice to find something more meaningful, a career. Then, comes the desire to do something even more meaningful—Life Work.*
> **—Diana Randolph, author, poet, and artist living out her True North as an art studio director.**

For you to make a critical career decision, you will want to carefully read real time job postings for different types of health science careers. To determine how well a career path fits your Directional Forces, you need to decode or break down the job description. You decode a job description in the same manner you decoded a class assignment in Chapter V. The purpose of decoding is the same—you are seeking to identify what Learning Processes are required for you to be successful in a specific career field.

> *Taking the time now to understand yourself as a learner will save you time as you move through your academic and professional career. This is because you will have the tools to make informed decisions. You will have the tools to tackle difficult tasks. You will have the tools you need to navigate in the direction you truly want to go.* —Nicole MunozMunoz, former businesswoman who found her True North as a teacher of young learners.

A typical job description begins by listing the title of the position followed by a listing of the education, certification, and job experience required. In the example that follows, the skill set required is listed immediately after the general requirements is listed. Do not ignore its content. Read it critically. To fail to decode this portion of the job description is to miss a key aspect of what the position entails. In the example that follows, the skills listed for the med lab technician focus on the use of very specific Directional Forces:

Skills Sought:
As our PST Specialist, you will need to demonstrate the ability to:

- Interact with patients and play a role in their overall healthcare experience.
- Follow directions without deviation.
- Maintain a schedule of routine services.
- Record data accurately.
- Work with new electronic reporting and accuracy tools, allowing you to focus on your patients and increase your success rates.
- Label, pack, and ship specimens for processing accurately following all DEA requirements and OSHA protocols.
- Interact daily with patients in a thoughtful and caring manner. This will be essential to your success.

If you decode these skills, you find a significant amount of Sequence is called for, a small but targeted amount of Precision is needed, a limited amount of Technical Reasoning is called for, and a tiniest use of Confluence is required:

Sequence   Interact (social interaction, discussion, social exchange)
Play a role
Follow directions
Maintain a schedule
Routine services
Follow labeling, packaging, and shipping requirements
Follow protocols
Focus on patients x 2

Precision   Report accurately
Accuracy
Label
DEA and OHSA protocols (specific protocols)

Technical Reasoning
Work with electronic equipment and accuracy tools
Pack specimens

Confluence (Contribute positively to) the patient's overall experience

Once you have decoded a typical job description within your area of interest, you need to compare your Directional Forces to those required to gain a reasonable understanding of the match between your Learning Processes and those required to fill the position. Now take this example a step further and apply it to your career interest. What is the match between your learning Compass Rose and different aspects of the career?

Pre-employment activities

Decoding a career path or specific job description is only one of many ways to make Critical Decisions about your future career. Gaining accurate information about the career you are seeking can be achieved through a series of pre-employment activities such as job shadowing or internships. One of the most effective is the informational interview.

The informational interview allows you to gain first-hand insight into a career you are exploring from a person who currently holds a job in your field of interest, a real "insider." By meeting with someone who has first-hand experience, you become more fully aware of the daily responsibilities and challenges of the job, and gain perspective about the realities of the career from someone who is living it. People who request informational interviews want knowledge and information about real-life experiences beyond what they have read in a book or heard about from a career counselor. The informational interview helps you to determine whether a specific career might be a good fit for you. It also allows you to develop your interview skills as you interact with your host.

Finding the right person for the informational interview is key. Contact family members, friends, friends of friends, or individuals you have read about in local business news publications to help you identify the best candidate for the interview. If you are enrolled in courses, communicate with your instructors in order to gain their expertise and input. Ask if they know of someone you could reach out to. Keep your interactions professional; the contacts you make during this process help lay the groundwork for future employment, as you'll be building a network of people who know that you are actively seeking a career in a specific area.

Once you have secured names, request appointments with these people, clarifying with each that the purpose is to conduct an informational interview, not a job interview. Most people enjoy talking about their jobs and genuinely want to help college students find their way, so they are receptive to informational interview requests.

After the appointments are scheduled, begin to gather information about the role each of your interviewees plays within his or her organization, as well as information about the organization for which each works. The informational interviews can provide you with "dress rehearsals" for actual job interviews, since the preparation is similar, in that for both, you must dress and act the part of a professional job seeker, and for both, you must do your "homework" and know about the specific job position you are seeking to explore as a career choice (Matthews, 2013). The difference is that in this case, you are driving the interview, and, in doing so, you are learning how to acquire information in a manner that works best for you.

For example, if you have strong Sequence and Precision Patterns, you may arrive at the interview with a systematic set of questions, beginning with, "Could you describe the structure of a typical day at work?" You might follow up with, "What actions comprise your typical work day? Writing directives? Communicating with clients? Problem-solving employee issues?" On the other hand, you don't want to over plan your questions or pack too much into the interviewee's limited time. Leave some time for the interviewee to open up topics you weren't aware of in advance. You may find these quite revealing.

However, if you Avoid Precision, you will need to prepare your questions in advance and have someone stronger in Precision check them over to make certain that they will elicit the type of information you are seeking, instead of simple yes-or-no answers that don't lead to much insight or invite follow-up questions.

The same is true for interviewers who Use Technical Reasoning First. While you may want to "cut to the chase" by beginning the interview with straightforward, practical questions, you might find your interviewee responds better to one or two warm-up questions that establish a cordial communication exchange before getting down to the essential information you have come to gather.

On the other hand, if you Use Confluence First and Avoid Sequence or Precision, you will want to develop an interview protocol that keeps you on target and focuses on asking the questions that are essential to the purpose of the informational interview. By preparing your list of questions and a brief list of general areas of conversation in advance, you'll stay on track while gaining relevant information.

You may want to consider the Learning Processes of the person you are interviewing and send the individual a courtesy copy of the questions in advance. By doing so, you give the person an opportunity to use his/her critical skills to prepare thoughtful responses with sufficient detail that they might not otherwise be able to produce on the spot.

Providing the questions in advance can also allow the interviewee to see you as a professional who is thoughtful, prepared, focused, and career ready. Depending on his or her Learning Patterns, your host may feel more comfortable with time to think about answers in advance. You will also want to take the initiative to attach your résumé to the questions so that the person you are interviewing has an opportunity to learn about your background prior to your arrival. One other thought: while your primary purpose for the informational interview is to gain insight into a career you're considering, your host may remember you for a future job opening or may know of someone who is looking for a new employee. Every opportunity for interaction helps build your job hunting toolbox and grows your network of contacts.

Of course there are an entire series of pre-employment activities you can use to help hone your Critical Decision-making skills. One of the most important is preparing your Intentional Résumés and Interviews. All career development pathways lead to the development of a résumé, and while the development of this skill may be in the distant future, it is important to note that when you do compose one, it should be developed by using your Learning Patterns with intention, and it should represent the finest use of your Critical Thinking, Critical Reading, Critical Writing, and professional ethical standards. It should represent you accurately, neither inflating your academic achievement, work experience, and skill set, nor under representing all you bring to a specific career opportunity.

The most recent study of employment recruiting trends reported by Michigan State University's Collegiate Employment Research Institute leaves no doubt that Critical Thinking, Critical Reading, and Critical Writing abilities affect an individual's chance to secure and hold a professional position. According to the study, employers are seeking individuals with meaningful work experience and the maturity to manage themselves and to deal with situations they will face as employees. Employers are also seeking individuals who have a command of the skills that allow them to converse with diverse colleagues and handle multiple assignments (Gardner, 2012, p. 30). The same study identified the following critical areas of performance that employers find lacking in many applicants:

Critical Reading: Often the résumés received don't match the posted position. "'Many of the résumés we receive are not tailored to the job; many people do not research my company and are not prepared for the interview,' said one frustrated human resources exec" (Gardner, 2012, p. 30). Obviously, the candidate who has not read the posting carefully or done accurate research about the company is unlikely to be of much interest to a recruiter.

Critical Writing: "I cannot begin to describe the atrocious writing style I see in cover letters and résumés and the lack of basic knowledge and skills in just Microsoft Office from new grads" (Gardner, 2012, p. 30). As one respondent in the study stated, "We need people who know how to write professional documents, communicate in a professional manner, and have a basic knowledge of how a professional organization acts" (Gardner, 2012, p. 31). Too frequently, a candidate's résumé is filled with errors in grammar, mechanics, usage, and style—and sometimes even incorrect contact information. Such résumés rarely receive more than a few seconds of a recruiter's time. Creating an effective résumé and cover letter requires the skillful crafting of its content so that its match to a specific job opening and its authenticity are obvious to the person reviewing it.

Critical Thinking Skills: Employers want résumés that authentically represent the candidate. Adjectives such as innovative, motivated, and results-oriented ring hollow within the interview setting unless they can be backed up with specific examples that are relevant to the position being sought. As another study participant asserted, ". . . touring a school-based health center for class does not make you an expert on how they function, but they are writing on their cover letters that they are EXPERTS" (Gardner, 2012, p. 30).

Additionally, even candidates whose skills span a broad spectrum of experiences frequently do not interview well because they have not used their Critical Thinking skills to prepare with intention for the interview. Employers also contend that many candidates look good on paper but have such "poor interpersonal skills and little or no understanding of what companies are looking for in candidates" that they are unprepared to relate their skills and experiences in a manner that illustrates their readiness to fit into the organization's culture and work ethic (Gardner, 2012, p. 30).

Critical Thinking, reading, writing, and decision-making skills play a vital role in your success in obtaining the position you have identified as your career goal. Read every posting critically, decoding it to see if it matches your Learning Patterns, interests, and skill set. If it seems a good match, compose your cover letter and résumé using Critical Writing skills and include terms and descriptive words that authentically match your goals, skills, and experiences with those the employer is seeking.

Take the risk (Confluence) to share your cover letter and résumé for feedback with no fewer than three professionals working in your desired career field. Use their feedback to help you think critically about how to articulate your thoughts (Precision) and present yourself during an interview. Give yourself the time to rehearse and reflect on your readiness (Sequence). Above all else, work with intention (Technical Reasoning) to bring your career goal to fruition.

Boxing the Compass

- The primary challenge facing individuals in the 21st-century global community is how to use the critical skills of thinking, reading, writing, and decision-making to learn ever more effectively and efficiently.
- A second challenge is understanding how the Directional Forces of your Compass Rose prepare for success in college and career.

Taking Stock

Use your Critical Thinking, reading, writing, and decision-making skills to complete the following assignment:

- Identify your career goal.
- Write a detailed description of what knowledge, skills, and training the career requires.
- Decode the career description.
- Compare your Directional Forces (a description of your Compass Rose of Directional Forces) with those called for in your description.
- Use your Personal Learning Profile (a description of your Compass Rose of Directional Forces) and your True North (your life focus) to compose a cover letter and resume that provide a potential employer with value-added insights of what you would bring to the workplace (See Figure 7.3 and Worksheet 7.1). How could preparing your employment application in this manner make your application standout from the others?

Key Questions for Critical Reading

What are you to know after reading the materials?	What is being written about? A story? A situation? An explanation of a real world phenomenon? An explanation of a process? (Precision)
	How does what you read unfold? From beginning to end? Through flashbacks? If you read about a science process or a history of something, what drives the process described in the reading? (Sequence)
	Who, what, where, and when? Why? (Precision) How does it work? How was it formed? How does it operate? Are there diagrams to read and interpret? Graphics with labels? Numbers? (Technical Reasoning and Precision)
	What is the central idea behind the passage? (Confluence and Precision) What new terms will you need to record, look up, and log for review? (Sequence and Precision)
How does the material prompt you to draw inferences and connect to existing knowledge?	What did you learn from a previous reading assignment that you can apply to this assignment? (Sequence and Precision) What is being suggested or inferred, but not actually stated in the material? (Confluence) What information is implied that you feel comfortable assuming is accurate because you have read something previously on a related topic? (Sequence and Precision) Johnston, 2012

Table 7.3: Key Questions for Critical Reading

Resume Outline with Embedded Directions

Name
Address
Dependable email   *(Develop a professional email address)*
Dependable phone number   *(Make certain your greeting is appropriate and professional)*

Position sought: *Take the title for the job right from the job description and place it here. Do not write a general objective. Be specific and let the employer know this is the job you are seeking.*

Education: *List your educational accomplishments including*
- *Diplomas*
- *Certifications (HazMat; OHSA, software etc)*
- *Licenses (CNA, CMA, EMT)*
- *Specialty training from military service or other*

Experience: *List the most current job held that relates specifically to the job you are currently seeking*
- *Use bullets to briefly identify what your specific responsibilities were.*
- *Be brief and accurate; do not overstate or understate your experience.*

Next list the other jobs you have held always adding bullets beneath each to explain what you did and the skills you used to accomplish the work of that job. Point out the transferrable skills gained from other employment that can apply to this position.

Workplace Skills*   *Read the job description, select key words that describe what the employer is looking for in an employee. Then match those key words to your Directional Forces and list them indicating how well you match what the employer is looking for. For example if your LCI scores show that you Use Sequence, Precision, and Technical Reasoning at the Use First level, you might write something like the following:*
- *I exhibit strong organizational skills which I use to set goals, schedule workload, meet benchmarks, and achieve outcomes,*
- *I maintain a neat work area and respect the workspace of others.*
- *I read and follow directions, improvise when directions are sketchy, and remain flexible if the original plans require a redesign.*
- *I am a problem-solver and can work interactively with a team, in tandem with others, or independently of others if necessary.*
- *I articulate my thoughts and information best when given the opportunity to prepare. I am not an "off the cuff" or "shoot from the hip" person. I prefer time to weigh information in the balance and then draw conclusions after discussing my findings with colleagues.*
- *I possess strong writing and speaking skills but prefer to speak from prepared notes rather than extemporaneously.*

*As documented by the Learning Connections Inventory (LCI) (Date completed).

Worksheet 7.1a: Resume Outline with Embedded Directions

Resume Outline

Name
Address
Dependable email
Dependable phone number

Position sought:

Education:

Experience:

Workplace Skills*

*As documented by the Learning Connections Inventory (LCI) (Date completed).

Worksheet 7.1b: Formatted Resume (blank)

PART IV
Finding Your Way:
Setting the Course

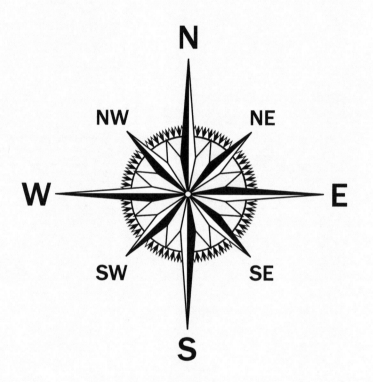

VIII. THE REPRISE

"I'm doing what I think I was put on this earth to do. And I'm really grateful to have something that I'm passionate about and that I think is profoundly important."
—Marian Wright Edelman (2008)

The Focus

- *Revisiting your True North*
- *Affirming the role learning plays in achieving success in the 21st century*

Every individual, regardless of geographic location, gender, race, color, or class, has the capacity to learn. Across the globe, the technology of the brain-mind and the Directional Forces that comprise our Compass Rose, equip us to learn. Learning, however, is not just global: it is also very personal! Learning is both a universal experience and a very personal experience. Again and again, we are reminded of the central role our True North and our Compass Rose play in our ability to achieve success in the 21st century. While the technology that connects the world is powerful; the technology of learning is more powerful. The technology of the mind that fuels learning is powerful because it is central to our individual personhood.

> *Learning is both a universal experience and a very personal experience.*

- It defines who we are and how we behave;
- It defines how others perceive us and interact with us;
- It develops our capacity and molds our future.

After reading the stories that comprise this text, you surely noted that individuals throughout history (inventors, scientists, writers, leaders, common laborers, young and old) have struggled to understand their learning selves and thus have suffered the consequences of not knowing how to respond appropriately to the learning challenges that confronted them:

- To recognize the True North of their lives and
- To acknowledge and use with intention their individual Directional Forces

The key difference between previous generations and us is that you and I now have the knowledge to understand our learning selves and can use that understanding to navigate our lives. We do not need to begin our learning journey ill equipped. We can use an Advanced Learning System that assists us in understanding and using our Compass Rose with intention to succeed in life. We know our True North and the Directional Forces of our Compass Rose, and therefore, are equipped to meet the challenges the future holds for us. We have the tools by which to explore, discover, and plot our life course so that, regardless of our destination, we are assured of success!

> *"To laugh often and much; to win the respect of intelligent people and the affection of children; to earn the appreciation of honest critics and endure the betrayal of false friends; to appreciate beauty; to find the best in others; to leave the world a bit better, whether by a healthy child, a garden patch or a redeemed social condition; to know even one life has breathed easier because you have lived. This is to have succeeded."*
> — **Ralph Waldo Emerson**

affectation This mental process focuses on our emotive response to a learning task, including our feelings of worth and value as learners.

Assess The phase of metacognition during which the learner confronts questions internally about what has been achieved and to what degree he or she has succeeded.

Attend How a learner pays attention to continuing to develop the strategies that brought him or her to a new level of achievement in order to maintain that new level.

Avoid LCI scale scores that range from 7 to 17 for a certain Pattern. When an individual avoids a Pattern, he or she will feel stress whenever asked to use that Pattern without the benefit of intentional strategies.

brain-mind connection
The relationship between the physiological structure of the brain, which processes stimuli in each human body, and human consciousness, which is not physically limited.

brain-mind interface The patterned processes that operate as a filter of stimuli passing from the brain to the mind. These filters welcome, inhibit, or limit the movement of stimuli as they seek to enter the working memory to be translated into language, numerals, etc., and directed into any number of memory channels, where they are stored for later retrieval and use.

Bridge learner A learner whose LCI scale scores fall between 18 to 24 in all four Patterns and can apply each Pattern on a Use as Needed basis.

chatter/internal chatter The internal communication among your Learning Processes as they interact and vie with one another for attention.

cognition Our internal processing of information. This mental process focuses on thinking, knowing, and understanding and retaining knowledge, data, and facts.

compass rose A directional symbol on a map indicating the four ordinal points of North, South, East, and West.

Compass Rose of Learning An individual's ordinal Directional Forces of learning: Sequence, Precision, Technical Reasoning, and Confluence. (See Learning Patterns/Learning Processes/ Directional Learning Processes/ Directional Forces.) .

conation The pace, skill, autonomy, and manner in which we perform a task. This mental process focuses on the doing of a learning task.

Confluence The Learning Pattern that describes the way we use our imagination, take initiative and risks, and brainstorm ways of approaching things in a unique manner. Confluence allows the learner to link disparate pieces of information into the big picture.

Connect After mulling and decoding the assignment accurately, a learner begins to generate and observe links between his or her own prior experiences and existing knowledge and the requirements of the task and content of required reading.decoding Analyzing a task to determine the degree to which

Glossary

each of the four Patterns is required to complete the task successfully. Used as a way for learners to determine how to apply their Patterns (i.e.,tether, intensify, or forge their use).

critical reading The skills used to dig deeply into text and thoughtfully identify the message of the prose, the quality of the research, and the accuracy of its content.

critical thinking The logic and reasoning you use to conduct a thoughtful and reasoned life, one based on principled decisions.

critical writing A piece of writingthat articulates your thoughts, opinions, perspectives, and arguments in a clear and logical manner.

Decoding Analyzing a task to determine which combination of the four Processes is required to complete the task successfully. These are used as a way for learners to assess how to apply their Learning Processes or Directional Forces (i.e., Tether, Intensify, or Forge their use).

deep reading A person's ability to intuit and understand the unspoken (written) message being conveyed beyond the written word; deep reading involves capturing the full meaning of the intent of the writer's message.

defining decisions Decisions a person makes that point to his/her use of critical thinking and that mark him/her as an individual who does not make decisions casually or without a basis of knowledge, skill, and principles. (See also principled choices.)

Directional Forces (See Learning Patterns).

Directional Learning Processes (See Learning Patterns).

Directional Tools The skills and materials that help individuals use their Directional Learning Processes with intention such as the LCI, personal Compass Rose, description of personal Compass Rose, the Word Wall, the Metacognitive Drill, FIT, work site strategies, and the personal Directional Forces Strategy Card.

Drivers A set of rules for ordering our lives instilled in us by parents and authority figures; these scripted messages consist of unachievable expectations that grow to be the drivers of our behavior as adults: Be Perfect, Please Me, Try Hard, Hurry Up, and Be Strong.

Dynamic learner The LCI scale scores of an individual who uses one or two Patterns at the Use First level and any other combination of Avoid or Use as Needed for the remaining Patterns.

Express To go public with what you have mulled, connected to, rehearsed, and attended to; to turn in your paper, to make your presentation, or take a test, after going through the first four phases of metacognition.

FIT/FITing Matching an individual's Learning Patterns to a specific task by using personal strategies to forge, intensify, and tether those Patterns to the specific level of use required by the task.

Forge Increasing the use of a specific Learning Pattern that an individual usually avoids in order for that person to succeed in completing a specific task. Forging requires intention, strategies, and focused energy.

informational interview Interviewing an individual who holds a responsible position within the career area of your choice and who is willing to share his or her knowledge, experiences, and expertise to help you determine whether working in that field is a good fit for you.

Intensify Increase the use of an individual's Use as Needed Pattern. Intensifying requires intention, strategies, and focused energy.

intentional learning Making the learning experience work for the individual by decoding the task, matching the individual's Patterns to the task, and then strategizing how to use the individual's Patterns to meet the requirements of the task.

job shadowing Spending a day or several days in the workplace with someone whose job you would like to learn more about; it gives a student an insider's look into the day-to-day career world and provides first-hand insights into a job.

Learning Connections Inventory (LCI) The instrument (a two-part, 28-question, self- report tool with three open-response written questions) that is administered to identify an individual's combination of Learning Patterns.

learning Our ability to take in the world around us and make sense of it so that we can respond to it in an efficient, effective, and appropriate manner.

Learning Patterns (Directional Forces/Directional Learning Forces/ Directional Learning Processes/ Learning Processes/Patterns used interchangeably) refer to Sequence, Precision, Technical Reasoning, and Confluence as they make up a person's Compass Rose of Learning.

Let Me Learn (LML) An Advanced Learning System A system for developing intentional learners. The system includes (1) a specific learning theory (the Brain-Mind Connection); (2) learning tools (the Learning Connections Inventory [LCI], the Learner Profile, the Word Wall, the Metacognitive Drill, and the Strategy Card); (3) a specific glossary of terms; and (4) skills for decoding, metacognating, and matching Learning Patterns to a task.

mental processes The cognition (thoughts), conation (action), and affectation (feelings) occurring in each Learning Pattern.

metacognition Traditionally, thinking about one's thinking. In the context of LML, it refers to the ability to hear the talk (sometimes referred to as internal chatter) among one's Learning Patterns and respond to the talk by using personal strategies to intervene and respond.

Metacognitive Drill The eight terms LML uses to explain what the learner is experiencing as he or she is completing a learning task.

Glossary

These terms include (1) Mull, (2) Connect, (3) Rehearse, (4) Attend (5) Express, (6) Assess, (7) Reflect, and (8) Revisit.

Metacognitive Process The phases of internal talk (internal chatter) that occur among an individual's four Patterns or Directional Learning Forces as he or she completes a task.

mindful Using the mind to attend, focus, and respond to stimuli with intention rather than instinct.

Mull(ing) Considering and contemplating the description or directions of an assignment until the learner is able to understand the expectations of the task and how he or she can make a conscious effort to begin his or her learning.

network(ing) Getting introduced to and building relationships with people who can help you progress in your career.

patterned operations The means by which the mind receives and processes stimuli from the brain, using the synchronous interaction of the four pattern filters of Sequence, Precision, Technical Reasoning, and Confluence.

Personal Learning Profile A record of one's Learning Patterns described in one's own words; a way of translating the Pattern scores into an authentic profile of the learner.

Precision The Learning Pattern that seeks information and details, asks and answers questions, and researches and documents facts.

range The range or degree of use of each Pattern: Use First (score 35–25), Use as Needed (score 24–18), or Avoid (score 17–07).

Reflect An inwardly directed activity that reinforces the ownership of the individual's learning strategies and intentional behaviors. This metacognitive phase follows assess and is the heart of becoming an intentional learner.

Reflective Practice Reflective practice is an inward directed activity that requires the individual to take ownership of his/her learning behaviors. This activity asks, "What were my assumptions as I entered the task? How did I expect things would occur? What did I or did I not do that resulted in this learning outcome? What would I do differently before I engage in a similar task?" .

Rehearse Privately practicing a response to a learning task. The only audience (and critic) is the learner himself or herself.

Revisit Considering the original learning task, a similar task, or an extension of that task (a new assignment) and applying what was learned through the metacognitive phases of assess and reflect.

scale scores An individual's numerical LCI scale scores, ranging from 7 to 35 on each Learning Pattern, that indicate to what degree an individual uses each Pattern. Typically expressed in the following order: Sequence, Precision, Technical Reasoning, and Confluence.

self-regulation Skills such as conscientiousness, self-discipline, and perseverance, as well the ability to consider the consequences of actions when making decisions.

Sequence The Learning Pattern that needs to organize, plan, and complete work assignments without interruption, using clear instructions as well as a time frame that allows for checking work.

strategy card A card on which a learner has written strategies identifying specific actions he or she can take in order to forge, intensify, or tether certain Learning Patterns in order to complete a task successfully.

Strong-Willed learner A learner whose LCI scale scores are 25 or more in at least three out of four Patterns.

team metacognition The intentional use of all of Learning Processes to approach any task as a joint effort combining the perspectives, thoughts, actions, and feelings of each Directional Learning Force into a single, focused, unified effort.

Technical Reasoning The Learning Pattern that describes the way we seek relevant real-world experiences and practical answers. This is the Pattern of the fewest words. It emphasizes the ability to problem-solve using independent, private thinking and hands-on interaction.

Tether Restrain the use of a Use First Learning Pattern. This is done with intention to allow the learner's other Patterns to operate more effectively.

true north An individual's driving passion or motivation in life—the goal toward which the individual strives, measures life-long fulfillment, and commits significant energy to achieve. It is the defining purpose which drives an individual over the course of a life time.

Use as Needed LCI scale scores that range from 18 to 24 for a certain Pattern.

Use First LCI scale scores that range from 25 to 35 for a certain Pattern. Learners use this Pattern first and begin their learning task relying on it.

Word Wall A tool to assist in decoding; it is a chart divided into four sectors, each labeled with a different Learning Pattern and a list of cue words that, when they appear in an assignment, indicate that that Pattern is required.

working memory The memory function that receives stimuli that have passed through the interface of our Learning Patterns and now require translation into symbolic representa- tion (words, numbers, musical notes, and the like), as well as intentional storage for ready retrieval.

References and Suggested Readings

Angelou, M. (2009). *I know why the caged bird sings.* New York, NY: Ballantine Books.

Bacon, F. (2010). *Essays or counsels—Civil and moral.* Retrieved. May 1, 2007, http://bacon.classicauthors.net/ EssaysOrCounsels CivilAndMoral/ EssaysOrCounselsCivilAndMoral.

Bennis, W. (2009). *On becoming a leader* (Fourth ed). New York: Basic Books.

Bruer, J. (1997). *Schools for thought: A science for learning in the classroom.* Cambridge, MA: MIT Press.

Christopherson, R. (2012). *Pilot study in brain-mind interaction with college text sample.* (Unpublished report) Arizona State University, School of Computing, Informatics, & Decision Systems Engineering, Tempe, AZ.

Collins, J. (2001). *Good to great: Why some companies make the leap . . . and others don't.* New York: HarperCollins.

Davies, P. (2007, March 11). *Einstein's god. Speaking of faith.* Paul, MN: NPR WHYY.

Dyson, F. (2007, March 11). *Einstein's god. Speaking of faith.* St.Paul, MN: NPR WHYY.

Edelman, Marian Wright. Interview with Marian Wright Edelman Founder and President, Children's Defense Fund. (2008, October 31). Retrieved from: http://www.kauffman.org/what-we-do/ articles/2008/10/interview-with-marian-wright-edelman-founder-and-president-childrens-defense-fund.

Friedman, T. (2005). *The world is flat: A brief history of the twenty-first century* (Updated and expanded version). New York, NY: Farrar, Straus and Giroux.

Friedman, T. (2006). *The world is flat: A brief history of the twenty-first century* (Updated and expanded version). New York: Farrar, Straus and Giroux.

Gardner, P. (2012). *Recruiting trends 2012–2013.* East Lansing, MI: Career Services and the Collegiate Employment Research Institute.

Grandin, R.(2007). Personal communication. April 14.

Hallowell. E. M. (2007). *CrazyBusy: Overstretched, overbooked, and about to snap. Strategies for handling your fast paced life.* New York: Ballantine Books.

Jha, A. P., Stanley, E. A., & Baime, M. J. (2010). What does mindfulness training strengthen? Working memory capacity as a functional marker of training success. In R. Baer (Ed.), *Assessing Mindfulness and Acceptance Processes in Clients: Illuminating the Theory and Practice of Change* (pp. 207–221). New York: New Harbinger Publications.

Johnston, C. (1994, September). *The interactive learning model.* Paper presented at the meeting of the British Education Research Association, Oxford University, Queen Anne's College, Oxford, United Kingdom.

Johnston, C. (2005, September). *Communicating from the inside out.* Keynote presentation at the National Writing Conference, Tumas Dingli School, Hal Warda Street, Attard, Malta.

Johnston, C. (2006). *Promoting mindful learning in the mindless school.* Keynote presentation at the Let Me Learn International Conference, Sunshine Coast University, Queensland, Australia.

Johnston, C. (2010). *Finding your way: Navigating life by understanding your learning self.* Printed by CreateSpace.

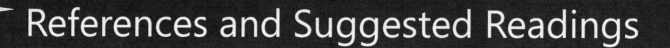

Johnston, C., & Dainton, G. (1994). Death by classroom: The perpetrator and the victims. In J. Rowan (Ed.), *Occasional papers on collaboration in education* (pp. 53-66). Vineland, NJ: Standard.

Johnston, C., & Dainton, G. (1996). *Learning connections inventory manual.* Thousand Oaks, CA: Corwin Press/Sage Publications.

Johnston, C., & Dainton, G. (2005). *The learning connections inventory manual.* Turnersville, NJ: Learning Connections Resources.

Kahler, T. (1977). The miniscript. In G. Barnes(ed.),Transactional analysis after Eric Berne. New York: Harper Row.

Kounios, J., & Jung-Beeman, M. (2006). Aha! favors the prepared mind. *Psychological Science.* Retrieved from www.psychologicalscience.org/media/releases/2006/pr060329.cfm

Lehmkuhle, S. (2011). Personal communication. November 2.

Lovett, M. (2008). *Teaching Metacognition.* Presentation at the Educause Learning Initiative 2008 annual meeting. Retrieved from http://net.educause.edu/upload/presentations/ELI081/FS03/Metacognition-ELI.pdf

MacLean, P. (1978). *A mind of three minds: Educating the triune brain.* In the 77th yearbook of the national society for the study of education. Chicago: University of Chicago Press.

Marzano, R. (1992). *A different kind of classroom: Teaching with dimensions of learning.* Alexandria, VA: ASCD.

Matthews, D. A. (2013, January). *3 ways to draw industry specific terminology on your resume.* Retrieved from http://www.illinoisjobnetwork.com/a/t-3-ways-to-draw-industry-specific-terminology-on-your-resume-au-debra-ann-matthews-articles-a6675.html

Munoz, N. (2015). Personal communication. January 25.

National Institute for Literacy. (2001). *Equipped for the future.* Retrieved from http://eff.cls.utk.edu/fundamentals/

National Work Readiness Council. (2006). *Getting ready for the work readiness credential: A guide for trainers and instructors of jobseekers.* Washington, D.C.

Nuland, S. (2007). *The biology of the spirit.* Retrieved from http://www.speakingoffaith.publicradio.org/programs/biologyofthespirit/transcript.shtml - 2007-01-18.

Ornstein, R., & Thompson, R. (1984). *The amazing brain.* Boston, MA: Houghton Mifflin Company.

Osterman, K. F., & Kottkamp, R. B. (2004). *Reflective practice for educators: Improving student learning* (2nd ed.). Newbury Park, CA: Corwin.

Paul, R., & Elder, L. (2001). *Critical thinking: Tools for taking charge of your learning and your life.* Upper Saddle River, NJ: Prentice Hall.

Postman, N. (1990, October). *Informing ourselves to death.* Conference of German Informatics Society (Gesellschaft fuer Informatik), Stuttgart, Germany.

Randolph, D. (1999). *In the heart of the forest.* Superior, WI: Savage Press.

Rose, M. (2004). *The mind at work: Valuing the intelligence of the American worker.* New York, NY: Penguin.

Schilpp, A. (1979). *Albert Einstein—Autobiographical notes.* Chicago University Press.

Senge, P.M. (1990). *The fifth discipline: The art & practice of the learning organization.* New York: Doubleday.

Senge, P. M. (1999). *The dance of change: The challenges momentum in learning organizations.* New York: Doubleday.

Smiles, S. (1884). *Men of invention and industry.* London: John Murray.

Snow, R., & Jackson, D. (1992). Assessment of conative constructs for educational research and evaluation: A catalogue. Washington, D.C.: U.S. Department of Education, Office of Educational Research and Improvement.

Sobel, D. (1996). Longitude: The true story of a lone genius who solved the greatest scientific problem of his time. New York: Penguin.

Useem, M. (1998.) The leadership moment: Nine true stories of triumph for all of us. New York: Three Rivers Press.

Suggested Readings

Johnston, C. (1996). **Unlocking the will to learn**. Thousand Oaks, CA: Corwin Press.

Johnston, C. (1997). *Using the learning combination inventory.* Educational Leadership, 55(4), 78–82.

Johnston, C. (1998). *Let me learn.* Thousand Oaks, CA: Corwin Press.

Olson, K. (2012). I *Learned to Believe in Me.* Educational Horizons, 90(3),10-13.

Wolf, M. (2009). *Proust and the squid: The story and science of the reading brain.* New York, NY: Harper Perennial.

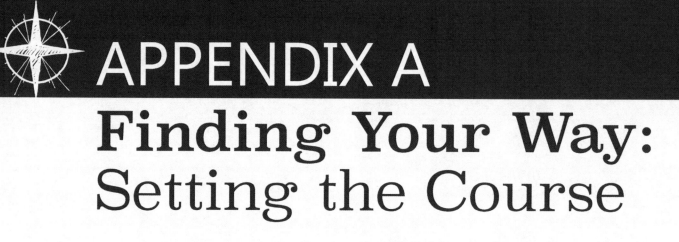

APPENDIX A
Finding Your Way:
Setting the Course

LEARNING CONNECTIONS INVENTORY (LCI)

DIRECTIONS FOR SCORING THE LCI

DIRECTIONS FOR VALIDATING THE LCI

TYPICAL SHORT ANSWER
WRITTEN RESPONSES

LCI Learning Connections Inventory

Making Connections/Developing Insights/Enhancing Relations

Learning Connections Inventory

Education Form II

Christine A. Johnston
Gary R. Dainton

Learning Connections Resources, LLC

Making Connections/Developing Insights/Enhancing Relations

The journey of learning never leaves us. We are in a constant search to understand our relationships, our experiences, and ourselves. The LCI is a tool dedicated to assist you by providing a voice, a language, and an appreciation of your personal learning connections.

For additional information or support contact:

Learning Connections Resources, LLC
PO Box 8861
Turnersville, NJ 08012-8861
USA
(856) 307-7878
www.LCRinfo.com

Education Resources:
Education Form I (Years K-4): ISBN#0-9754826-0-2
Education Form II (Years 5-12+): ISBN#0-9754826-1-0
Education Adult Form (Adults engaged in education): ISBN#0-9754826-2-9

Family Resources:
Kids Form I (Years 6-10): ISBN#0-9754826-4-5
Kids Form II (Years 11-18): ISBN#0-9754826-5-3
Adult Form (Years 18+): ISBN#0-9754826-6-1

Professional Resources:
Professional Form (For working adults): ISBN#0-9754826-3-7

For more information about using the LCI in education environments please visit:
Let Me Learn, Inc
2 Tiverstock Dr.
Pittsgrove, NJ 08318
(856) 358-0039
www.letmelearn.org

Education Form II

Learning Connections Resources

You have probably been told many times that learning is an important part of life. Something parents and teachers may not have told you is that each one of us has his or her own special way of learning that helps us to think and understand, work and perform, develop and mature as successful students.

Your answers to the following statements can help you and your teachers, parents, and friends understand how you personally connect with learning.

 Learning Connections Inventory

Learning Connections Inventory

Name: _____

There are three parts to the Learning Connections Inventory.
- Part I begins on page three. In this part you are asked to respond to 28 different statements by selecting your answers from the five choices.
- Part II begins on page seven. In this portion you are asked for a written response to three questions.
- Feel free to begin with either Part I or Part II.
- After completing Parts I and II, complete Part III on page eight.

Part I
This is a way to find out about how you accomplish learning tasks. There are 28 statements each followed by five phrases which read: *"never ever," "almost never," "sometimes," "almost always," and "always."*

Directions
Here is what you are to do. **1)** Read each sentence carefully. **2)** Decide how well it connects with how you learn. **3)** Circle the phrase that matches what you decided. Be sure that you circle only one phrase for each statement. **4)** Complete the three short answer questions to the best of your ability. Write as much or as little as you feel until you feel you have answered the question.

Let's Practice!

Sample Statements

A. I like to listen carefully when the teacher is giving directions.

B. I like to stand in the front of the class and act out skits or plays.

Words of Encouragement: Take the time you need and consider your responses carefully. While there are no right or wrong answers, there are answers that are more accurate to who you are than others. Selecting answers from each category provides a more accurate picture of your specific learning processes.

Choosing answers is not always easy. Often, if you decide on your answer, you will select "Sometimes" as a compromise. Rather than doing this, we encourage you to change the wording in a sentence or add to the wording so that you can select a response from the continuum that specifically describes you. Feel free to write any changes in the booklet. Most importantly, have fun, relax, and enjoy learning more about yourself.

1. I would rather build a project than read or write about a subject.

NEVER EVER	ALMOST NEVER	SOME- TIMES	ALMOST ALWAYS	ALWAYS

2. I need clear directions that tell me what the teacher expects before I begin an assignment.

NEVER EVER	ALMOST NEVER	SOME- TIMES	ALMOST ALWAYS	ALWAYS

3. I generate lots of unique or creative ideas.

NEVER EVER	ALMOST NEVER	SOME- TIMES	ALMOST ALWAYS	ALWAYS

4. I memorize lots of facts and details when I study for a test.

NEVER EVER	ALMOST NEVER	SOME- TIMES	ALMOST ALWAYS	ALWAYS

5. I feel better about an assignment when I double check my answers.

NEVER EVER	ALMOST NEVER	SOME- TIMES	ALMOST ALWAYS	ALWAYS

6. I like to take things apart to see how they work.

NEVER EVER	ALMOST NEVER	SOME- TIMES	ALMOST ALWAYS	ALWAYS

7. I am interested in detailed information about whatever I am studying.

NEVER EVER	ALMOST NEVER	SOME- TIMES	ALMOST ALWAYS	ALWAYS

3

8. I like to come up with a totally new and different way of doing an assignment instead of doing it the same way as everybody else.

NEVER EVER	ALMOST NEVER	SOME- TIMES	ALMOST ALWAYS	ALWAYS

9. I prefer to take a paper and pencil test to show what I know.

NEVER EVER	ALMOST NEVER	SOME- TIMES	ALMOST ALWAYS	ALWAYS

10. I keep a neat notebook, desk, or work area.

NEVER EVER	ALMOST NEVER	SOME- TIMES	ALMOST ALWAYS	ALWAYS

11. I like to work with hand tools, power tools, and gadgets.

NEVER EVER	ALMOST NEVER	SOME- TIMES	ALMOST ALWAYS	ALWAYS

12. I am willing to risk offering new ideas even in the face of discouragement.

NEVER EVER	ALMOST NEVER	SOME- TIMES	ALMOST ALWAYS	ALWAYS

13. I need to have a complete understanding of the directions before I feel comfortable doing an assignment.

NEVER EVER	ALMOST NEVER	SOME- TIMES	ALMOST ALWAYS	ALWAYS

14. I find that reading information is my favorite way to learn a subject.

NEVER EVER	ALMOST NEVER	SOME- TIMES	ALMOST ALWAYS	ALWAYS

4

15. I like hands-on assignments where I get to use mechanical/technical equipment.

      NEVER   ALMOST   SOME-   ALMOST   ALWAYS
      EVER   NEVER   TIMES   ALWAYS

16. I become frustrated when I have to wait for the teacher to finish giving directions.

      NEVER   ALMOST   SOME-   ALMOST   ALWAYS
      EVER   NEVER   TIMES   ALWAYS

17. I prefer to build things by myself without anyone's guidance.

      NEVER   ALMOST   SOME-   ALMOST   ALWAYS
      EVER   NEVER   TIMES   ALWAYS

18. I become frustrated if directions are changed while I am working on the assignment.

      NEVER   ALMOST   SOME-   ALMOST   ALWAYS
      EVER   NEVER   TIMES   ALWAYS

19. I keep detailed notes so I have the right answers for tests.

      NEVER   ALMOST   SOME-   ALMOST   ALWAYS
      EVER   NEVER   TIMES   ALWAYS

20. I don't like having to do my work in the way the teacher says, especially when I have a better idea I would like to try.

      NEVER   ALMOST   SOME-   ALMOST   ALWAYS
      EVER   NEVER   TIMES   ALWAYS

21. I clean up my work area and put things back where they belong without being told to do so.

      NEVER   ALMOST   SOME-   ALMOST   ALWAYS
      EVER   NEVER   TIMES   ALWAYS

5

22. I enjoy the challenge of fixing or building something.

NEVER EVER	ALMOST NEVER	SOME-TIMES	ALMOST ALWAYS	ALWAYS

23. I react quickly to assignments and questions without thinking through my answers.

NEVER EVER	ALMOST NEVER	SOME-TIMES	ALMOST ALWAYS	ALWAYS

24. I enjoy researching and writing factual reports.

NEVER EVER	ALMOST NEVER	SOME-TIMES	ALMOST ALWAYS	ALWAYS

25. I ask more questions than most people because I just enjoy knowing things.

NEVER EVER	ALMOST NEVER	SOME-TIMES	ALMOST ALWAYS	ALWAYS

26. I like to figure out how things work.

NEVER EVER	ALMOST NEVER	SOME-TIMES	ALMOST ALWAYS	ALWAYS

27. I am told by others that I am very organized.

NEVER EVER	ALMOST NEVER	SOME-TIMES	ALMOST ALWAYS	ALWAYS

28. I like to make up my own way of doing things.

NEVER EVER	ALMOST NEVER	SOME-TIMES	ALMOST ALWAYS	ALWAYS

6

Education Form II

Part II

Answer each of the following questions using the space provided. Write as much as you need until you feel comfortable that you have answered the question.

1. What makes school assignments difficult for you?

_____

_____

_____

_____

2. If you could choose, what would you do to show your teacher what you have learned?

_____

_____

_____

_____

3. What hobby or sport do you do well? How would you teach someone else to do it?

_____

_____

_____

Learning Connections Inventory

SCORING SHEET

Name: _____

Score the responses for Questions 1-28 using a 1 for "never ever," 2 for "almost never," 3 for "sometimes," 4 for "almost always," and 5 for "always." Next, transfer the score of each response to the center of the corresponding circle below. Add up the inserted numbers and record the total in the space at the end of each line. Transfer your total for each pattern to the bar graph at the bottom of the page.

PATTERNS	2	5	10	13	18	21	27	TOTAL
Sequential Processing	○	○	○	○	○	○	○	_____

	4	7	9	14	19	24	25	
Precise Processing	○	○	○	○	○	○	○	_____

	1	6	11	15	17	22	26	
Technical Processing	○	○	○	○	○	○	○	_____

	3	8	12	16	20	23	28	
Confluent Processing	○	○	○	○	○	○	○	_____

Your Learning Connections

Graph the totals from each of the lines above on the appropriate bars below.

PATTERNS | I avoid this pattern. | I use this as needed. | I use this pattern first.

7   12   17   21   25   30   35

Sequential Processing
Precise Processing
Technical Processing
Confluent Processing

Education Form II

Printed in the United States of America

©Learning Connections Resources, LLC 2003

9

Learning Connections Resources
PO Box 8861
Turnersville, NJ 08012-8861
USA
(856) 307-7878
www.LCRinfo.com
ISBN#0-9754826-1-0

Making Connections/Developing Insights/Enhancing Relations

SCORE: 1 2 3 4 5

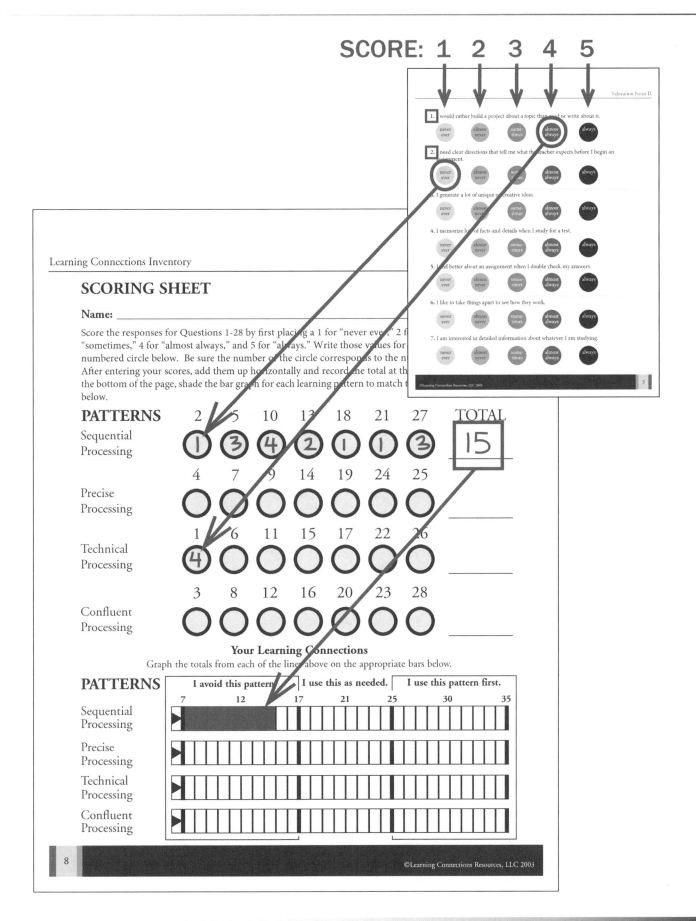

Education Form II

1. would rather build a project about a topic than read or write about it.
   never ever · almost never · some-times · almost always · always

2. need clear directions that tell me what the teacher expects before I begin an assignment.
   never ever · almost never · some-times · almost always · always

3. I generate a lot of unique or creative ideas.
   never ever · almost never · some-times · almost always · always

4. I memorize lots of facts and details when I study for a test.
   never ever · almost never · some-times · almost always · always

5. I feel better about an assignment when I double check my answers.
   never ever · almost never · some-times · almost always · always

6. I like to take things apart to see how they work.
   never ever · almost never · some-times · almost always · always

7. I am interested in detailed information about whatever I am studying.
   never ever · almost never · some-times · almost always · always

©Learning Connections Resources, LLC 2003   3

Learning Connections Inventory

SCORING SHEET

Name: _____

Score the responses for Questions 1-28 by first placing a 1 for "never ever," 2 for "sometimes," 4 for "almost always," and 5 for "always." Write those values for numbered circle below. Be sure the number of the circle corresponds to the n After entering your scores, add them up horizontally and record the total at th the bottom of the page, shade the bar graph for each learning pattern to match t below.

PATTERNS	2	5	10	13	18	21	27	TOTAL
Sequential Processing	①	③	④	②	①	①	③	15

	4	7	9	14	19	24	25	
Precise Processing	○	○	○	○	○	○	○	____

	1	6	11	15	17	22	26	
Technical Processing	④	○	○	○	○	○	○	____

	3	8	12	16	20	23	28	
Confluent Processing	○	○	○	○	○	○	○	____

Your Learning Connections
Graph the totals from each of the lines above on the appropriate bars below.

PATTERNS	I avoid this pattern	I use this as needed.	I use this pattern first.

7   12   17   21   25   30   35

Sequential Processing ▶

Precise Processing ▶

Technical Processing ▶

Confluent Processing ▶

8   ©Learning Connections Resources, LLC 2003

Observe the match between the content of the short answers and the scores of the Learning Processes.

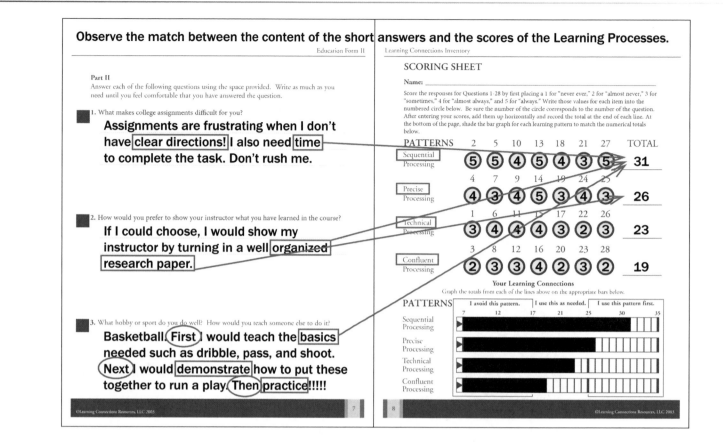

Education Form II

Part II
Answer each of the following questions using the space provided. Write as much as you need until you feel comfortable that you have answered the question.

1. What makes college assignments difficult for you?

Assignments are frustrating when I don't have clear directions! I also need time to complete the task. Don't rush me.

2. How would you prefer to show your instructor what you have learned in the course?

If I could choose, I would show my instructor by turning in a well organized research paper.

3. What hobby or sport do you do well? How would you teach someone else to do it?

Basketball. First I would teach the basics needed such as dribble, pass, and shoot. Next I would demonstrate how to put these together to run a play. Then practice!!!!!

©Learning Connections Resources, LLC 2003   7

Learning Connections Inventory

SCORING SHEET

Name: _____

Score the responses for Questions 1-28 by first placing a 1 for "never ever," 2 for "almost never," 3 for "sometimes," 4 for "almost always," and 5 for "always." Write those values for each item into the numbered circle below. Be sure the number of the circle corresponds to the number of the question. After entering your scores, add them up horizontally and record the total at the end of each line. At the bottom of the page, shade the bar graph for each learning pattern to match the numerical totals below.

PATTERNS	2	5	10	13	18	21	27	TOTAL
Sequential Processing	⑤	⑤	④	⑤	④	③	⑤	31

PATTERNS	4	7	9	14	19	24	25	
Precise Processing	④	③	④	⑤	③	④	③	26

PATTERNS	1	6	11	15	17	22	26	
Technical Processing	③	④	④	④	③	②	③	23

PATTERNS	3	8	12	16	20	23	28	
Confluent Processing	②	③	③	④	②	③	②	19

Your Learning Connections
Graph the totals from each of the lines above on the appropriate bars below.

PATTERNS	I avoid this pattern.	I use this as needed.	I use this pattern first.
	7 12	17 21	25 30 35
Sequential Processing			
Precise Processing			
Technical Processing			
Confluent Processing			

8   ©Learning Connections Resources, LLC 2003

134

Typical Written Comments by Individuals Who Use
a Directional Force at a Use First Level

SEQUENCE	PRECISION	TECHNICAL REASONING	CONFLUENCE
Clear Directions	**Correct Information**	**Technical Reasoning/ Hands-on**	**Use My Own Ideas**
I become frustrated when the directions aren't clear or don't make sense. I don't work well when I don't have good instructions or the instructor doesn't do a good job of explaining the assignment. I hate it when the instructor keeps changing the directions in the middle of the assignment.	I want to know specifically what will be on the exam so I can study all the details. I'm frustrated when I don't know all the answers because I like being right. I am frustrated when I don't have enough information or I can't find the information and the answers aren't in the text.	I want hands-on activities that interest me instead of reading, taking notes, or writing about it. Give me the tools and let me demonstrate what I know hands-on. Let me build things!	I am frustrated when I feel trapped in the instructor's ideas. That's when I don't even feel like doing the assignment. I am frustrated when I come up with a certain idea, and I'm not allowed to use it. I don't like having to do an assignment in one certain way.
Practice/Planning	**Detailed Information**	**Autonomy/ Being Outside**	**Use of Imagination**
It's hard when the instructor isn't organized or doesn't explain things thoroughly. I like the instructor to go slow and make sure everybody is at the same spot. I always practice my answers by going over and over them. I like plenty of in-class practice.	I become frustrated when the instructor doesn't go into detail and explain things. Confusion! I would have students take notes and do activities to reinforce the information. I take detailed notes and then go over and over them. I like trivia. I'm good at that.	I need to get outside of the classroom to get things to make sense in my head. I need to take lots of breaks when studying. Let me learn by going home and living and experiencing it. I don't let the instructor know what I know. I am a very private person. I keep it inside.	I need to be allowed to use my imagination! I like exploring new things. I like to work with people who are curious and don't do assignments in just one way. Let students learn however they want.
Time to Complete Work	**Asking/Answering Questions**	**Real-World Experiences**	**Presentation/Creative Writing**
I don't like it when I don't have enough time to do an assignment thoroughly. I'm frustrated when the instructor gives us lots of work and no time to do the work. I need time to complete my work and double-check it. I need time to make my work neat with no eraser marks.	I like to show people what I know by answering all the instructor's questions. If you want to know what I know, read my answers or ask me questions. I write down what I want to say so when I speak I say things correctly.	I learn better from real-world experiences. Take me out into the real world and show me something. I learn by living what I learn. I learn better if I can do what I am learning about. Give me a real challenging project with a point to it and let me figure it out.	I like to write about things using the same voice I'd use if I were telling someone something face to face. I like writing stories using my own ideas. I like to stand up and speak without rehearsal. I don't like having to do an assignment in one certain way.

Appendix A: Directional Force at Use First Level

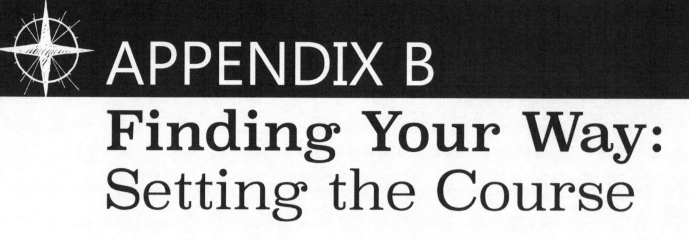

APPENDIX B
Finding Your Way:
Setting the Course

ADDITIONAL LML WORD WALLS

MATH

WORKPLACE

Math Word Wall

Sequence

- categorize
- follow step-by-step routines
- formulate
- repeat numbers in sequence
- note geometric symmetry
- observe sequencing patterns
- organize data
- repeat
- sort numbers into categories
- systematize information into a grid, table, or diagram
- use algorithms

Precision

- add
- be accurate
- calibrate
- compute
- correct
- count
- define
- divide
- fact find
- inform
- measure
- memorize mathematical definitions
- multiply
- record information
- subtract
- test a solution for correctness

Technical Reasoning

- apply mathematical theorems
- build a grid, table, or diagram
- check for feasibility
- deconstruct solutions check for feasibility
- diagram
- draw 3-dimensional shapes in 2-dimensional space
- manipulate (rotate, flip, or move) shapes in the mind
- solve
- reason
- reassemble solutions
- use number facts

Confluence

- draw conclusions based upon a variety of data
- estimate an amount
- find new ways to solve problems
- formulate an untested theory
- find new ways to solve problems
- guess
- hypothesize
- imagine
- imagine a 3-dimensional shape based on a 2-dimensional image
- posit
- predict
- vary (variables) (variety)
- work backwards or out of sequence

Appendix B: Math Word Wall

Workplace Word Wall

Sequence

- adhere to policies
- alphabetize
- arrange
- bullet
- classify
- compare and
  contrast
- develop
- direct clients
- distribute
- follow directions
- format
- frame or structure
- maintain records
- review
- schedule
- sequence
- sort and label
- use spreadsheets
- schedule

Precision

- answer questions
- calibrate
- calculate
- classify (label)
- code
- communicate
- describe
- document
- examine
- explain
- evaluate
- identify
- identify
  pros and cons
- inform
- label
- manage records
- measure
- meet deadlines
- name
- observe
- retrieve data
- record data
- specify
- verify and complete
  required documents
  and reports

Technical Reasoning

- assemble
- build
- construct
- demonstrate
- design
- draft (blueprints)
- engineer
- erect
- experience
- figure out
- fix
- implement
- handle hazardous
  materials
- just do it!
- problem solve
- operate concretely
- represent graphically
- utilize hand held
  devices
- use motorized
  equipment
- safely walk, climb,
  push, bend, squat
- use appropriate
  tools safely
- work independently
- write concisely

Confluence

- brainstorm
- concoct
- create
- consider
  alternatives
- dream-up
- experiment
- go beyond the
  limits
- imagine
- improvise
- innovate
- invent
- originate
- push the envelope
- remain flexible
- risk
- take a chance
- think outside the
  box
- take a calculated
  risk

APPENDIX C
Finding Your Way: Setting the Course

HOW TO DEVELOP
PERSONAL STRATEGIES

Starter Strategies

The following chart of Forge and Tether strategies is intended to help you develop your own set of strategies.

Begin by placing your Directional Force scores above the appropriate column for Sequence, Precision, Technical Reasoning, and Confluence. If the score of a particular Learning Process falls in the Avoid Range (07-17) or low Use As Needed (18), look down the column and check off those strategies you believe can assist you in using that Process with greater intention. If, on the other hand, your score for a particular Process falls in the Use First (25-35) or high range of Use As Needed (24), turn to the Tether strategies found on the next page. Proceed to read down the column of suggested strategies and check off those that seem appropriate to the typical assignments you are asked to complete.

Experiment with the strategies you have checked. Eventually you will want to reword these in order to make them your own.

How to Develop My Own Personal Strategies

SEQUENCE	PRECISION	TECHNICAL REASONING	CONFLUENCE
Forge Strategies	**Forge Strategies**	**Forge Strategies**	**Forge Strategies**
___ read the directions carefully.	___ take my time and carefully read over all of the information.	___ be willing to show others what I know by demonstrating something or building it.	___ think of something unusual for real life and then stretch it to be imaginary.
___ mark off each step as I go.	___ read the subtitles to know where to gather information.	___ use whatever tools that are given to me to show what I know.	___ be willing to take small risks with new ideas.
___ look for words that ask for me to respond using a specific order or organization.	___ don't trust my memory; and write it down!	___ remind myself that I can learn from experiences, so observe and absorb the experience as it is occuring.	___ be willing to do a skit with other people to show what I know.
___ double check my work for completeness.	___ look for words that ask for important facts or details.	___ look to see if I can work with someone who uses technical as needed.	___ take my time to think of ways to do assignments in a unique or different way.
___ make sure that I follow the key directions step-by-step.	___ answer questions using at least two full sentences.	___ look for words that ask me to build or make something.	___ ask others for ideas to get started.
___ make sure that I do not start something until I have all of the directions or unless I have permission to try a different approach.	___ double check my work for accuracy.	___ think about how I can apply this to my life.	___ be willing to learn about things in creative, fun, and entertaining ways.
___ work to follow through with one project from beginning to the end.	___ whenever possible, ask questions about things I am not sure of.	___ stick with the task until I can make it work.	___ look to see if I can work with someone who uses confluence as needed.
___ look to see if I can work with someone who uses sequence as needed.	___ look to see if I can work with someone who uses precision as needed.		___ work to make connections in order to see the big picture.

Appendix C: How to Develop My Own Personal Strategies

SEQUENCE	PRECISION	TECHNICAL REASONING	CONFLUENCE
Tether Strategies	**Tether Strategies**	**Tether Strategies**	**Tether Strategies**
___ when the directions aren't clear think of an assignment that was similar to the current task and make up your own directions.	___ answer the question first and add detail if there is time.	___ take short breaks to refresh and keep motivated.	___ remember that not everyone likes change.
___ think through the steps carefully before asking what I am to do	___ remember that not everyone communicates in words.	___ remember that I can communicate using words.	___ don't get discouraged if my idea is not used.
___ take a deep breath when plans change and take the risk not to be in control for the moment.	___ think about the question before I ask. Sometimes I already know the answer (trust myself).	___ know that when I work with others they have something to teach me too.	___ make sure to follow the assignment's objectives and if I'm not sure, ask.
___ when there is a time limit, don't panic; place a star by the most important areas that need to be double-checked.	___ remember to allow others to share their information.	___ try to connect with the task faster rather than mulling for a long period of time.	___ work to not wait until the very last minute. This will give me time to make corrections and allow it to be more complete.
___ remember that not everyone has the same plan as me.	___ don't get hung-up on mistakes. Correct them and move on.	___ remember that I have something that is valuable to teach others.	___ allow others to share their opinions.
___ allow wait time for others to respond.	___ remember that there are times when I don't have to prove my point.	___ if I can't get it to work and there's a time limit, ask for help.	___ remember that others may need help "seeing" my idea and its connections to the task.
___ don't panic when the final product doesn't look like the example.	___ seek to prioritize the amount of information that needs to be shared out loud or on paper.	___ keep in mind that not everything has a purpose or has to work.	___ stick to the task, don't let my mind wander.
			___ remember to rehearse before I express.

Appendix C: How to Develop My Own Personal Strategies

Finding Your Way:
Setting the Course

SAMPLE CLASS ASSIGNMENT

PHYSICS 100 LAB

Decoding Phys 100 Lab #1   Name:_____

Once you know your combination of Learning Patterns, you can then develop strategies to help you cope with the learning tasks, project assignments and work responsibilities that you encounter in college. This process will help you become an Intentional Learner. Central to becoming an Intentional Learner is mastering the technique of Decoding.

> Decoding is analyzing the assignment or task in terms of what Learning Patterns will be required to successfully complete the task.

An efficient method for Decoding a task is to use the Word Wall to *identify* key words in the description of the task so that you can *identify the Learning Patterns that will be essential to completing the task.*

1) Using the Word Wall shown below, underline the Learning Pattern key words in the following lab exercise description:

Experiment D: More Measurements
Without laying a meter stick end-to-end, make whatever measurements you think are needed to determine the length and width of this lab room. Make a sketch of the room to help you, labeling the major dimensions. Put your final answers in units of meters. Give a brief explanation of what measurements you made and how you calculated the room dimensions. As always, record your answers to the proper precision.

Sequence Cue Words		Precision Cue Words	
alphabetize	order	accurately	facts
arrange	organize	calibrate	identify
classify	outline	certainty	label
develop	plan	describe	measure
distribute	put in order	detail	observe
group	sequence	document	record
in a series	show a sample	exact	specific
list	show an array	examine	write
		explain	

Technical Reasoning Cue Words		Confluence Cue Words	
assemble	erect	brainstorm	improvise
calculate	experience	carefree	incredible
brief	figure out	create	independence
build	graphically	different	invent
concrete	represent	dream-up	risk
construct	just do it	far fetched	take a chance
demonstrate	problem solve	ideas	unique
draw (drafting)	tools	imagine	unusual
engineer	visualize		

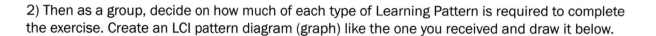

2) Then as a group, decide on how much of each type of Learning Pattern is required to complete the exercise. Create an LCI pattern diagram (graph) like the one you received and draw it below.

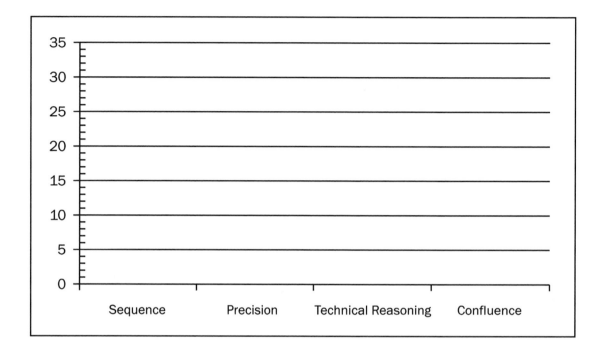

3) Identify the degree to which you are going to be required to use your Patterns in a manner different from your normal use in order to accomplish the task. Will you need to increase or decrease a type of Learning Pattern to successfully complete the lab exercise? Explain.

4) Now share your LCIs with group members and discuss any issues that may occur as you work together to complete the lab exercise. Summarize your discussion.

About the Author

Dr. Christine A. Johnston, originator and lead researcher of the **Let Me Learn Process**, an advanced learning system, has an abiding passion for helping people to understand themselves as learners and to improve their learning and their relationships with others.

During Christine's academic career in higher education she served in two capacities: professor in the Department of Educational Leadership at Rowan University, Glassboro, NJ, and later as Director of the Center for the Advancement of Learning where she conducted K–16 research on learning. Her professional life has also included managing the State of Illinois Department of Local Government Affairs Internship and Urban Planning Programs, consulting with corporate and educational leaders, and developing workforce training and management programs for primary school and adult learners in the United States, the United Kingdom, Central Europe, the Mediterranean Rim, and Australia.

She has authored and coauthored numerous books on learning, communication, and the Let Me Learn Process as well as numerous articles, videos, and book chapters. In 2010 she published *Finding Your Way: Navigating Your Life by Understanding Your Learning Self*, as a guide for professionals to achieve greater success and fulfillment in personal and professional lives. Educators, students, job trainers and other professionals and individuals have used the self-guided text worldwide. In 2013 she authored *Intentional Learning for College Success* which has been used by over 25,000 students to increase their persistence and retention in higher education.

In this latest text, focused on collegiate learners, she is seeking to help students find greater success through knowing *how to leverage themselves as learners* in both the classroom and the work world.

Johnston earned her BA from the University of Wisconsin—Eau Claire, her MA from the University of Wisconsin—Milwaukee, and her Ed.D. from Rutgers University.

Index